The Seasonal Cookbook

DIANA AND PAUL PEACOCK

SPRING HILL

Published by Spring Hill, an imprint of How To Books Ltd
Spring Hill House, Spring Hill Road
Begbroke, Oxford OX5 1RX
United Kingdom
Tel: (01865) 375794
Fax: (01865) 379162
info@howtobooks.co.uk
www.howtobooks.co.uk

How To Books greatly reduce the carbon footprint of their books
by sourcing their typesetting and printing in the UK.

The paper used for this book is FSC certified and totally chlorine-free. FSC (The Forest Stewardship
Council) is an international network to promote responsible management of the world's forests.

British Library Cataloguing in Publication Data
A catalogue record of this book is available from the British Library.

ISBN: 978 1 905862 37 5

Produced for How To Books by Deer Park Productions, Tavistock, Devon
Designed and typeset by Mousemat Design Ltd
Edited by Jamie Ambrose
Printed and bound by in Great Britain by Ashford Colour Press, Gosport, Hants

NOTE: The material contained in this book is set out in good faith for general guidance and no
liability can be accepted for loss or expense incurred as a result of relying in particular circumstances
on statements made in the book. Laws and regulations are complex and liable to change, and readers
should check the current position with relevant authorities before making personal arrangements.

The Seasonal Cookbook

Visit our How To website at www.howto.co.uk

At www.howto.co.uk you can engage in conversation with our authors – all of whom have 'been there and done that' in their specialist fields. You can get access to special offers and additional content, but most importantly you will be able to engage with, and become a part of, a wide and growing community of people just like yourself.

At www.howto.co.uk you'll be able to talk and share tips with people who have similar interests and are facing similar challenges in their lives. People who, just like you, have the desire to change their lives for the better – be it through moving to a new country, starting a new business, growing their own vegetables, or writing a novel.

At www.howto.co.uk you'll find the support and encouragement you need to help make your aspirations a reality.

You can go direct to www.theseasonalcookbook.co.uk which is part of the main How To site.

How To Books strives to present authentic, inspiring and practical information in its books. Now, when you buy a title from **How To Books,** you get even more than just words on a page.

Contents

Introduction: The Heart of Seasonal Cooking

Try as you may, it is difficult to persuade anyone used to our modern way of purchasing food from a shelf or a freezer in a large supermarket about the superiority of eating seasonal food that is grown and harvested when nature intended. How can you, in words alone, explain the joy of fresh seafood in the spring? The mere thought of cockle salad or homemade pizza with hand-caught shrimps and mussels is enough to make you want to get to Morecambe Bay right now and start fishing.

Similarly, there is no pleasure known to man, no incentive, price or any other item, gift or experience better than a simple egg that has been collected within minutes of being laid, then poached carefully, or incorporated into a cake. All foods have their season, eggs included. The eggs we buy from the shops are usually a month old, by which great age they are just not the same, having lost what they were when they first popped out of the clucking hen.

It is beyond our ability to describe waiting for the first new potatoes of the year, and then eating them with nothing more than a bit of butter and a little pepper. Yes, you can buy young potatoes at any time of the year, but real, brand-new, dug-up potatoes that are then eaten at the peak of their flavour are another matter.

Seasonal cooking, using fresh produce – sometimes that you've grown yourself – teaches you about ingredients, their true flavours and how they behave in the pan. It is one thing cooking with the ingredients bought from a shop, but quite another cooking with really fresh produce.

Diana and I sat in an auditorium recently answering questions about bees and beekeeping, and the topic of why supermarkets sell strawberries in December came up. Quite what it had to do with bees is a mystery to me, but on the panel was an environmentalist employed by one of the UK's leading supermarket chains. His answer was frighteningly simple. 'If people want to buy strawberries for Christmas, we'll import them from wherever we can to meet that need.'

So it is down to the customer *not* to want strawberries for Christmas. How can you not want strawberries? It is one of the most popular flavours in the world, and almost everyone loves them. I, for one, am greedy with them: once they appear in the garden, I scoff the lot. I get protective on a grand scale and guard them against slugs and snails. If I happen to miss one and some wild creature eats it, I am driven mad with rage. But this 'natural greed' is not the same as overindulgence.

The value of the natural sweetness and flavour of the strawberry in June is undermined by those eaten between December and May. There is something about waiting for a flavour, an ingredient or some produce, that makes it all the sweeter when it finally arrives. And the wait *is* worthwhile; there is just no comparison between the flavour of home-grown strawberries eaten in June with their tasteless counterparts that arrive in the supermarkets in December. There are plenty of other things to eat at Christmas, so why not just wait and enjoy the anticipation of the June fruit?

There are more than just gastronomic reasons for eating seasonally. To take the supermarket spokesperson literally, eating what we want whenever we want it has a terrible effect on the planet. A punnet of strawberries bought in a supermarket in December is likely to have come from Kenya or Spain. The cost of transporting it here is reflected in the price of the strawberries, and this is so frighteningly little that one wonders what the farmer gets.

Yet there are more costs than just the financial ones. The planet pays in extra pollution to pack, encase, transport to an aeroplane, in the infrastructure to make the roads, in the vehicles themselves and also in the cost of fuel in bringing them thousands of miles to our shops. Everyone agrees this is unsustainable – but still we do nothing about it.

Walking from my kitchen door to my strawberry patch – five large strides – brings me strawberries in season: strawberries with no pesticides or chemicals added. Strawberries that have nothing but a positive effect on my whole day and are good for the planet, too.

You don't even need a garden to enjoy fresh seasonal produce. Nor do you have to be a flat-capped allotmenteer. Even a pot of carrots on the patio will broaden anyone's gastronomic horizons. And everyone is within reasonable distance of a market garden or a farm shop ready to sell the freshest of produce as it arrives from the fields. The difference between cabbage cut that morning and cabbage languishing first in a truck, then on a shelf for a few days is immense – and surely worth the effort of finding a really fresh supply?

Maybe you are close to one of the many box-delivery schemes? Usually run by smallholders, they are invariably packed with the best and freshest vegetables and fruit you could wish for, and frequently at a price that isn't that much different from the old stuff they sell in the supermarkets. Sometimes they provide vegetables you wouldn't have thought of using or can't readily get in the shops, such as celeriac. We tried our first celeriac from just such a scheme and now grow it ourselves.

These days, in order to survive in a great competitive war with supermarkets, butchers have proudly championed British and local meat. At my butchers, the only real one left in north Manchester, you can get rabbit shot in the fields the day before. How fresh is *that*? Like fresh fruit and veg, not only is the flavour of local, well-hung meat far superior to the meat you buy in the supermarket, but most butchers are only too happy to give you their expert advice on how to cook it.

Seasonal cooking and seasonal produce should, in our opinion at least, be everyone's experience. Certainly I can guarantee that once you've started enjoying fresh food according to season, you'll find it difficult to go back. And the planet, as well as you and your family, will definitely benefit from that 'difficulty'.

Paul and Diana Peacock

After the festivities of Christmas, January can sometimes feel dull and depressing, so it is important to make it special, spoil yourself and celebrate the New Year with good food.

Frost tempers the diet in January: we feel the need for 'real food'. Cold waters bring the best fish to our markets at this time of year. Molluscs are musclier and white fish appears cleaner and fresher, with flakes that hold together well on the fork and fall apart deliciously on the tongue. The reason behind all this is simply the cold. Those of us used to making wine understand that dissolving solids in water is a more efficient process when the water is warm. Gasses, however, dissolve more efficiently in cold water, and the colder it gets, the more oxygen dissolves. Consequently fish – the best fish – is caught in the icy cold waters of the January sea.

Similarly, frosted January plants are blessed with flavours that are simply not available in insipid winters, when constant rain makes them muddy and miserable. The colder garlic becomes, the stronger its flavour. Cabbage, broad beans, chicory, leek and spring onions each benefit from a good frosting, and this is due to yet another paradox of nature.

Normally, things shrink in the cold; they withdraw and protect themselves. Yet ice crystals expand. In plants, this expansion causes damage, and as a plant repairs itself, one of the by-products of the process is better flavour. A prolonged frost produces the best flavour in winter produce. Cabbages, onions and winter greens respond by creating plenty of sulphur-laden molecules – hence the flavour.

January

January Menu

A three-course meal to serve 4 people

Seared Scallops with White-wine Vinaigrette

Venison Tournedos Rossini with Celeriac Mash

Pancakes in Satsuma Sauce

Seared Scallops with White-wine Vinaigrette

This starter course is quick and easy. It should be prepared just before serving.

For the vinaigrette
2 tablespoons
  white-wine vinegar
2 tablespoons
  clear honey
½ teaspoon salt
2 tablespoons
  sunflower oil
2 teaspoons Dijon
  mustard

2 tablespoons oil and
  a knob of butter
12 large scallops –
  remove the corals
  if you wish
Salt and pepper
  to taste
12 medium
  chicory leaves

1. Make the vinaigrette by whisking all the ingredients together in a bowl or jug.

2. In a frying pan, heat the oil and butter together until hot. Add the scallops. Don't be tempted to move them about the pan; just leave them until they are ready to be turned. After about 2½ minutes, when they start to turn golden around the edges, turn them over and cook for another 2½–3 minutes. Season to taste.

3. Arrange the chicory leaves on each plate and place the cooked scallops on each of the leaves.

4. Drizzle over the dressing so that it covers the leaves and scallops thinly. Serve immediately.

Venison Tournedos Rossini with Celeriac Mash

Venison is so versatile because it can be cooked in many different ways. This is a speedy yet impressive dish – perfect to serve to guests at a dinner party.

Salt and pepper
  to taste
4 venison steaks, about
  8–9cm across and
  4cm deep
50g butter
4 large, flat mushrooms
150g very good duck
  or game pâté,
  sliced to fit on top
  of the venison
4 thick slices of bread,
  cut slightly larger
  than the meat

For the celeriac mash
1 small celeriac
25g butter
2 tablespoons cream
Salt and black pepper

1. Season the steaks on both sides. Melt the butter in a large frying pan over a medium heat and fry the steaks for 3–4 minutes each side, or to taste. Remove from the pan and keep warm.

2. Fry the mushrooms in the same pan until tender then keep warm.

3. Fry the pâté until it browns slightly, then place each slice on top of the warm steaks.

4. Fry the slices of bread in the same pan, gathering up all the flavours and juices. Turn to fry the other side. When the bread is crisp, put each slice on a plate, then top with the venison and pâté and finish with a mushroom.

5. Serve with the celeriac mash.

To make the celeriac mash
1. Peel and dice the celeriac and put in a saucepan with sufficient water to cover. Boil until tender – this will take about 15 minutes. Drain well.

2. Put back in the pan and add the butter, cream and seasoning to taste. Mash well until smooth.

3. Serve with the venison tournedos.

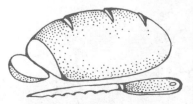

Pancakes in Satsuma Sauce

This is similar to crêpes Suzette, but uses satsumas and Grand Marnier. It goes wonderfully well with vanilla ice cream, but it is also good with cream.

For the pancakes
110g plain flour
1 tablespoon golden
 caster sugar
2 eggs, beaten
250ml milk
25ml orange juice
Zest of 3 satsumas
25g butter

For the satsuma sauce
8 satsumas, peeled,
 pith removed
1 teaspoon zest from
 the satsuma peel
100ml fresh
 orange juice
2 tablespoons
 caster sugar
3 tablespoons Grand
 Marnier or brandy
20g butter

1. Sieve the flour into a bowl, stir in the sugar and make a well in the centre. Add the beaten eggs and whisk them into the flour, gradually picking up the flour as you whisk.

2. When all the egg is incorporated, whisk in the milk a little at a time.

3. Add the orange juice and satsuma zest and whisk into the milk and flour mixture.

4. Melt the butter gently in a small pan. Remove from the heat.

5. Have a plate ready to hold the cooked pancakes, as well as about 8 sheets of greaseproof paper to lay between them so that they don't stick together.

6. Use a piece of kitchen paper to brush the base of of a small frying pan with the melted butter. Heat the pan until it is hot.

7. Turn the heat down to medium. Pour in sufficient batter – about 2 tablespoons – to just cover the base of pan. Allow this to set (about 30 seconds), then turn the pancake over and cook the other side for about the same time.

8. Use a spatula to transfer the pancake to the prepared plate.

9. Continue making and transferring the pancakes and place a sheet of greaseproof paper between each.

To make the satsuma sauce

1. Put 6 of the prepared satsumas in a blender and whizz for a few seconds. Strain the juice into a jug. Discard the solids.

2. Remove the flesh from each of the segments of the other 2 satsumas and set aside.

3. Mix the satsuma juice and zest and orange juice together with the sugar and spirit.

4. Melt the butter in a heavy-based frying pan and add the juice mixture. Heat the sauce gently. Fold the pancakes into quarters and add them to the sauce.

5. Add the satsuma segments and heat until everything simmers.

6. Serve on warmed plates with ice cream or a little cream.

Devilled Oysters

Some good, crusty bread makes the ideal accompaniment to this dish.

Serves 4 as a starter or snack, 2 as a main course

20 oysters (removed from their shells)
50ml white wine
Salt and pepper to taste
2 tablespoons double cream
100g wholemeal breadcrumbs
1 level teaspoon cayenne pepper
½ level teaspoon chilli flakes

1. Put the oysters in a saucepan. Pour in the wine and season to taste. Poach over a low heat until the oysters go lighter in colour; this will take about 3 minutes.

2. Place the oysters in a well-buttered shallow dish and boil the remaining liquor for about 4 minutes, or until it has reduced by half. Remove from the heat and stir in the cream. Pour this over the oysters.

3. Combine the breadcrumbs with the cayenne pepper and chilli flakes and sprinkle over the oysters.

4. Crisp the top under a grill for a minute or so until the topping is golden, but don't leave for long or the oysters will toughen. Serve immediately.

Cream of Brussels Sprout Soup

This delicious soup is an excellent way to serve sprouts to people who are not – or think they're not – so keen on them.

Serves 4

50g butter
1 large onion, chopped
300g potatoes, peeled
   and cut into
   approximately
   2cm chunks
Salt and pepper
   to taste
1kg Brussels sprouts,
   halved (or quartered
   if they are large)
800ml vegetable or
   poultry stock
200ml milk
A little grated nutmeg
100ml single cream

1. Melt the butter in a saucepan and fry the onions gently until they are soft.

2. Add the potatoes and season to taste with salt and pepper. Stir and allow the potatoes to cook gently for 5–6 minutes.

3. Add the sprouts. Cook for 2 minutes, then add the stock, milk and nutmeg.

4. Bring to the boil, then turn down the heat and simmer for 20 minutes. Remove from the heat.

5. Purée the soup in a blender (or use a hand blender) until the desired texture is achieved.

6. Reheat the soup and swirl in the cream. When hot, serve immediately.

Parsnip and Potato Cakes

These can be served on their own as a snack or with eggs and bacon, but they can also be served with steak instead of chips or boiled potatoes. If you like, this recipe can be made as one large cake, cut into wedges to serve.

Makes 6–8, depending on how large you want them to be

300g potatoes, peeled
280g parsnips, peeled
1 medium onion,
  finely chopped
½ teaspoon
  dried thyme
1 garlic clove,
  finely chopped
Salt and pepper
  to taste
1 egg, beaten
2 tablespoons oil,
  for frying
120g mature
  Cheddar, grated

1. Grate the potatoes and parsnips and put them in a sieve over a bowl. Gently squeeze out the excess moisture.

2. Put the onion in a mixing bowl. Add the potato and parsnip and mix well with the thyme, garlic and seasoning.

3. Stir in enough of the egg to bind all the ingredients together.

4. Using your hands, form the mixture into cakes and press down to flatten them.

5. Heat the oil in a frying pan and fry the cakes on a medium heat for 5 minutes.

6. Turn the cakes over and sprinkle with the cheese. Cook for 4–5 minutes more, or until golden and crispy around the edges.

7. Serve immediately or keep warm in the oven to serve with other food.

THYME

Parsnip Bread

The flavour of this bread is different to what you might expect. It isn't overwhelmed by the flavour of parsnips, but has a savoury yet sweet taste. Delicious served with soups of all kinds.

Makes 1 medium loaf

250g strong white flour (or a mixture of 150g white and 100g wholemeal)
½ teaspoon salt
1 sachet fast-action dried yeast
150g parsnips, peeled and grated; excess moisture squeezed out
100ml warm milk
20g butter, melted

1. Sieve the flour and salt together into a mixing bowl.

2. Stir in the dried yeast.

3. Add the parsnips and mix well.

4. Make a well in the centre and add the milk and melted butter.

5. Combine using your hands and begin to knead together. If the dough is too sticky, add a sprinkling of extra flour.

6. Knead for 10 minutes, then shape into a round cob and place on a greased baking sheet. Leave to prove in a warm place for about 30 minutes, or until it has doubled in size.

7. Preheat the oven to 220°C/gas mark 7.

8. Bake for 20 minutes. If after 10 minutes the crust is cooking too quickly, turn the heat down to 200°C/gas mark 6 and continue the cooking time.

9. Allow to cool before slicing.

Variation
Shape the kneaded dough into 8–10 small rolls and prove for 20–25 minutes. Bake for 10–15 minutes.

Pork Steak with Leek and Sage Sauce

A good winter warmer, especially when served with buttered carrots or sprouts and some baked potatoes.

Serves 4

Salt and pepper
  to season
4 lean pork steaks,
  each weighing
  about 150g
1 tablespoon oil

For the sauce
25g butter
2 medium leeks,
  chopped
1 garlic clove, chopped
4–5 chopped sage
  leaves or 1 level
  teaspoon dried sage
Salt and pepper
  to taste
100ml dry cider
3 tablespoons
  double cream

1. First, make the sauce. Melt the butter in a pan and fry the leeks gently for 4 minutes.

2. Add the garlic and sage, season to taste and continue frying until the leeks are soft.

3. Add the cider and stir. When the sauce is simmering, turn down the heat and allow to cook slowly.

4. Preheat the grill to a medium-to-hot setting.

5. Season the steaks with salt and pepper – but remember that the sauce is already seasoned – and brush each with oil. Place on a baking tray and grill for 4–5 minutes each side, depending on the thickness of the meat.

6. Add the cream to the sauce and stir, then remove from the heat.

7. When the steak is cooked, reheat the sauce if necessary. Serve the steak on warm plates with the sauce poured on top.

Leek and Cheese Savoury

This tasty supper dish can be served on its own or with pork sausages or bacon.

Serves 4

1kg potatoes
50g butter
3 leeks
Salt and pepper
   to taste
1 teaspoon
   chopped rosemary
200ml vegetable stock
100g breadcrumbs
150g mature
   Cheddar, grated

1. Peel and cut the potatoes into small chunks about 1.5cm in size. Boil in salted water for 4 minutes. Drain and leave to one side.

2. Melt the butter in a pan and fry the leeks, without browning, until tender.

3. Add the rosemary and stock and bring to the boil. Turn down to a simmer and add the potatoes. Cook for 3–4 minutes and season to taste with the salt and pepper.

4. Butter a heatproof dish and pour in the potato and leek mixture.

5. Mix the breadcrumbs and cheese together and spoon on top of the vegetables.

6. Grill for 3–4 minutes, or until the topping is golden and crispy.

Stuffed Winter Cabbage Leaf Casserole

A hearty casserole that goes very well indeed with bread or crispy potato wedges.

Serves 4

1 large onion, chopped
1 tablespoon oil
2 garlic cloves,
   chopped
250g minced pork
250g minced beef
½ teaspoon
   dried thyme
3 chopped sage leaves
400ml beef stock
Salt and pepper
   to taste
100g boiled rice
100ml white wine
8 large cabbage leaves
3 tablespoons
   tomato purée

1. Preheat the oven to 180°C/gas mark 4.

2. Cook the onions in the oil over a gentle heat. Make sure the onion doesn't brown.

3. Add the garlic and the meat and fry together until the meat has changed colour.

4. Stir in the herbs and about 50ml of the stock and season to taste. Simmer until the liquid has almost gone. Remove from the heat and stir in the rice.

5. Bring a pan of salted water to the boil and add the cabbage leaves. Turn off the heat and leave for 30 seconds. Drain the leaves.

6. Flatten the leaves carefully without them splitting and place an eighth of the meat mixture in the centre of each leaf. Fold in the sides and roll up like a parcel, then place each parcel, open edge down, into a buttered ovenproof dish. Put all the leaf parcels close together in the dish so that they don't unfold.

7. Mix the rest of the stock, wine and tomato purée together and pour over the cabbage parcels.

8. Cover and cook for 1 hour. Remove the cover and cook for 15 more minutes.

Mussels in Leek and White-wine Sauce

Serve this in a soup bowl as a starter with a crusty roll, or with pasta or rice as a main course. When preparing dishes with mussels, always discard any that are open and don't close when tapped.

Serves 4

50g butter
2 leeks, finely chopped
1 bay leaf
200ml dry white wine
150ml fish or
   vegetable stock
120ml double cream
Salt and pepper
   to taste
1.3–1.5kg mussels,
   cleaned

1. Melt the butter in a large pan and add the leeks. Fry gently until they are soft.

2. Add the bay leaf, the white wine and the stock and bring to the boil. Turn the heat down slightly and simmer for 5 minutes, then add the cream. Season with salt and pepper to taste.

3. Carefully add the mussels to the pan, lowering them in without breaking the shells. Bring the sauce back to boiling and cover.

4. Cook for 2–3 minutes, then check that all the mussels have opened. Discard any that haven't. Remove from the heat.

5. Put the mussels in bowls and pour over the sauce, or place the mussels on a bed of rice or pasta and pour over the sauce.

Variation
You could also use cooked shelled mussels in this recipe. At Step 3, add the prepared mussels and follow the rest of the recipe. You will need about 450g mussels to serve 4 people.

Baked Cod Fillet with Chard

This is an unusual and tasty way to serve white fish such as cod. You could also use pollack, haddock or coley.

Serves 4

4 cod fillets, each
   about 150g
About 2 tablespoons
   olive oil
Fresh ground black
   pepper and salt
   to taste
50g butter
2 large tomatoes,
   chopped
2 tablespoons tomato
   purée mixed with
   4 tablespoons water
2 teaspoons
   balsamic vinegar
1 teaspoon
   brown sugar
450 chard, chopped,
   thick stems removed

1. Preheat the oven to 180°C/gas mark 4.

2. Put the fish fillets onto a buttered baking tray, brush them with the oil and sprinkle with salt and black pepper. Bake for 15–20 minutes.

3. Melt the butter in a lidded pan over a low heat and fry the tomatoes until they begin to disintegrate into the butter.

4. Stir in the tomato purée, vinegar and sugar and cook for 3 minutes until everything is well combined.

5. Add the chard and raise the heat to simmering. Cover and cook for 3–4 minutes, or until the chard has wilted into the sauce but still has bite.

6. Spoon the chard and tomato mixture onto plates and place the fish on top. Serve with fried or Dauphinoise potatoes.

Dauphinoise Potatoes

A potato dish that almost cooks itself!

Serves 4

750g potatoes, peeled
and sliced thinly
Salt and black pepper
to taste
2 garlic cloves, grated
300ml double cream
100ml single cream

1. Preheat the oven to 160°C/gas mark 2. Butter a gratin-style ovenproof dish.

2. Put the slices of potato in the dish in layers and press them down.

3. Season with salt and pepper and dot evenly with the garlic.

4. Mix the creams together and pour over the potatoes. Use the back of a spoon to press the potatoes down.

5. Bake for 1–1¼ hours, or until the potatoes are tender and the top is golden brown.

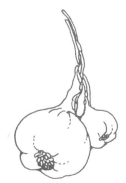

Sausage and Root Vegetable Cottage Pie

Not only a very easy and tasty version of the traditional recipe, but also very economical. It was first made when cottage pie was on the menu but there were only sausages in the freezer – so this is the result.

Serves 4

450g pork sausages
400g or 4 medium
    potatoes, peeled
    and cut into
    2cm chunks
1 large parsnip,
    peeled and cut
    into small pieces
2 medium
    carrots, diced
200g swede, peeled
    and diced
Salt and white
    pepper to taste
75g butter

1. Preheat the oven to 190°C/gas mark 5.

2. Cut the sausages in half on one side as far as the skin on the other side, then peel away the meat and discard the skins. Press the sausage meat down into an ovenproof dish or roasting tin.

3. Bake the meat in the oven for 10 minutes, then carefully pour off any excess fat (some sausages won't need this). Leave on one side until the vegetables are ready.

4. Put the vegetables in a large pan and add a teaspoon of salt and sufficient water just to cover them. Bring to the boil and cook until they are tender.

5. Drain well and put back in the pan with the butter and a little seasoning to taste; white pepper works well with root vegetables but use black pepper if you prefer.

6. Mash the vegetables roughly, leaving some chunks: this adds texture to the finished dish. Spoon on top of the meat and use a fork to put furrows into the top.

7. Bake in the oven for 20–25 minutes, or until the top is golden around the edges. Serve immediately.

Poached Pears with Easy Chocolate Sauce

The chocolate sauce used in this recipe is so quick and delicious, but the dessert can be served with ice cream as well.

Serves 4

For the pears
100ml water
100ml apple or
   pear juice
100ml pale
   cream sherry
60g golden
   caster sugar
2 tablespoons honey
1 teaspoon
   vanilla extract
½ level teaspoon
   cinnamon
4 pears, peeled,
   but leave the
   stalk on

For the chocolate sauce
100g dark chocolate,
   broken into
   small pieces
120ml evaporated milk

1. Put all the ingredients except the pears into a pan and bring up to simmering point.

2. Add the pears and simmer gently for about 35 minutes, or until the fruit is tender. Turn the pears in the liquor from time to time.

3. Place the pears in serving bowls or dishes and bring the liquor to the boil. Allow to reduce by half.

4. Pour the reduced liquor over each of the pears and serve with the chocolate sauce.

For the chocolate sauce
Put the evaporated milk in a small pan with the chocolate over a very low heat. Stir gently until the chocolate has melted into the milk. Serve either hot or cold.

Pear and Almond Cake

Serve hot with custard or cream, or slice it and serve it cold.

Makes 8–10 portions

175g butter
175g golden
    caster sugar
1 teaspoon
    vanilla extract
190g self-raising flour
2 eggs, beaten
½ teaspoon
    grated nutmeg
2 medium pears
Zest and juice of
    1 lemon
50g ground almonds
80g flaked almonds
1 tablespoon
    demerara sugar

1. Grease and line a 20cm springform cake tin. Preheat the oven to 180°C/gas mark 4.

2. Cream the butter and sugar together and add the vanilla.

3. When the creamed mixture is light and fluffy, add a tablespoon of the flour. Gradually beat in the eggs.

4. Sieve the flour and nutmeg into the creamed mixture and add the ground almonds. Fold everything in together.

5. Peel, core and slice the pears thinly. Sprinkle over the lemon juice and zest.

6. Spoon half of the cake mixture into the prepared tin, then spread the pears evenly over the top and spoon the rest of the mixture on top.

7. Scatter the flaked almonds over the top of the cake and sprinkle with the demerara sugar. Bake for 35-40 minutes until well-risen and springy to the touch.

Variation
For a stronger almond flavour, replace the vanilla extract with almond extract or essence. Use only ⅓–½ teaspoon because the flavour is much more intense than the vanilla.

Pear and Apple Jam

A lovely jam that should keep for up to one year. There is no need to peel the fruit, as the pectin lies in the layers just under the fruit skin. But if you prefer to peel it, then put the peel in a muslin bag and cook it along with the fruit and the sugar – and remove just before potting.

**Makes about
4 x 450g jars**

750g (diced weight)
  cooking apples,
  cored and diced
750g (diced weight)
  pears, cored
  and diced
Juice of 2 lemons
1kg sugar

1. Put a small plate in the fridge to cool so you can test for the setting point (see below).

2. Put the fruit in a large pan. Add the lemon juice and heat to simmering. Simmer for 4 minutes, then add the sugar and stir until the sugar has dissolved.

3. Bring to the boil and continue to boil for 15–20 minutes.

4. Remove from the heat while you check the setting point, using the cold plate as follows: drop a teaspoon of the jam into the centre of the plate and push it with your finger. If it wrinkles, it has reached setting point; if your finger makes a gap in the jam and it falls back together, it needs extra boiling time. If this happens, boil for another 3–5 minutes, then test again.

5. Ladle the jam into sterilised jars and seal well. Label with the type of jam and the date.

Seville Orange Marmalade

January is the time to make Seville orange marmalade because the oranges have a very short season. They make the best marmalade because they are very bitter, and when combined with sugar, their tangy orange flavour is still strong. Don't be alarmed by the amount of pips; they're not grown for their use as a dessert fruit!

**Makes about
8–9 × 450g jars**

1.5kg Seville oranges
2.5 litres water
Juice of 2 lemons
2.2kg sugar

1. Put a small plate in the fridge to cool so you can test for the setting point (see below).

2. Wash the fruit, cut each in half and squeeze out the juice into a pan. Put all pips in a dish ready to be tied in a muslin bag or square.

3. Scoop out all the pith and flesh from the oranges and put it in the pan. If there are some very thick bits of pith (most will dissolve in cooking and help the marmalade set), cut them away and put them in with the pips.

4. Cut the peel into thin strips —as thin as you like in your finished marmalade. Add these to the pan with the other orangey bits. Add the water and put the pips and pith bits in a muslin bag and tie well. Pop them in the pan also.

5. Bring to the boil, then turn down the heat and simmer for 2 hours until the peel is very soft. Remove the pips bag with tongs and squeeze out all the juice. It looks slimy, but this is the pectin being extracted.

6. Remove from the heat and stir in the lemon juice and the sugar. Put back on a low heat and stir until all the sugar has dissolved.

7. Bring to the boil and boil for 10 minutes. Test for the setting point: drop a teaspoon of the marmalade into the centre of the plate and push it with your finger. If it wrinkles, it's ready; if your finger makes a gap and it falls back together, it needs extra boiling time. If this happens, boil for another 3–5 minutes, then test again.

8. Leave to cool for 10 minutes, then stir to distribute the peel evenly. Ladle into sterilised jars, label and date.

Old English Marmalade

Makes about
8 x 450g jars

1.5kg Seville oranges
2.5 litres water
1kg white sugar
1.2kg brown sugar
1 tablespoon
  dark treacle

Prepare as in the Seville orange marmalade on the previous page, but after the sugar has dissolved, stir in the treacle and proceed in the same way.

Quick Pear and Onion Relish

If you fancy serving a delicious relish and time is short, try this recipe. It makes enough for about eight servings, but will keep in the fridge in a covered container for a week – if you have any left!

Makes 8 servings

250g onions,
   sliced thinly
½ teaspoon
   dried thyme
1 tablespoon
   balsamic vinegar
2 tablespoons
   white vinegar
3 tablespoons
   caster sugar
2 tablespoons water
2 pears, cored
   and chopped

1. Put the onions, thyme, vinegars, sugar and water in a pan and bring slowly to the boil, stirring to make sure the sugar dissolves.

2. When boiling, turn the heat down and simmer for 10 minutes.

3. Add the pears to the simmering mixture and continue to simmer for 15–20 minutes, or until the mixture has thickened.

4. Allow to cool completely before serving with grilled pork chops or steak or some good sausages and mash.

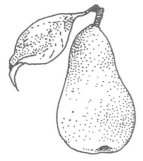

Pickled Beetroot

This will keep for up to two months. For a longer shelf life, use boiling vinegar; then it will keep for up to six months.

**Makes about
4 × 450g jars**

2kg beetroot
About I litre of spiced
    pickling vinegar
    (see recipe below)

**For the quick
    spiced vinegar**
I litre malt vinegar
Ready-mixed pickling
    spice: the correct
    amount to use
    should be on
    the packet

1. Wash the beetroot and put them in a pan. Add sufficient salted water just to cover and boil for about 1 hour (or until tender).

2. Cool, then rub off the loose skin – it should come off easily.

3. Either slice or dice the beetroot and pack it into sterilised jars. This is easier with diced beetroot.

4. Pour in the vinegar – enough to cover the beetroot with about 5mm on top.

5. If you like a sweeter pickle, sprinkle ½–1 teaspoon sugar into the vinegar and beetroot while in the jar. Cover with a secure lid. Label and date.

For the quick spiced vinegar
1. Put the vinegar in a double boiler or glass bowl over a pan of cold water. Add the pickling spice.

2. Bring to the boil, then remove from the heat but keep the vinegar bowl in the hot water so that they both cool down together.

3. Strain if you wish and use.

February is a month of hope, just as much as August is a month of passing. The planet, pulled by forces beyond human ken, turns sharply towards the sun – which is why, by the end of the month, the wind often responds with violence. In February there is a feeling that spring is on its way, but fresh fruit and vegetables are still low in variety. This doesn't mean boring food, however; with a little imagination great meals can be prepared and enjoyed. After all, this is the time of year that the last of the leeks and parsnips make wonderful soups.

Applying a cloche to the garden brings out all kind of vegetables, and of these, the very best is beet. Sow beetroot in November and you can have a wonderful treat in February, and the whole of the plant is edible. Leaves can be used in salads, whole shoots can be boiled like spinach, and the baby roots, not quite round but just as tasty, can be boiled and sliced, stir-fried or sautéed.

There are other foods around, if one knows where to look for them. To modern palates, the dandelion seems a bitter little plant fit for growing out of walls and pavement cracks, yet a hundred years ago you would have found them peeping through the soil in neat rows in everyone's garden. They made the very first salads of the year, and if you like endive (or rather, if you pay a fortune for endive), you'll love dandelion. Nettles are also at their best when they appear in late February, producing the best soup in the world; just remember to wear gloves when harvesting them.

Freezing nights, with more layers of clothing than can possibly be described, are best spent fishing for whiting. This underrated fish is really best fried there and then on the beach, but it's usually too cold at 4am on the harbour wall to operate matches or a lighter properly, so the catch is taken home after gutting it – a welcome treat for the gulls that wait greedily on the tops of the boats.

February

February Menu

A three-course meal to serve 4 people

❧

Broccoli Mornay

❧

Spicy Battered Hake with Parsnip Fries

❧

Rhubarb Crumble

Broccoli Mornay

A quick and easy starter or supper dish served with crusty rolls.

500g broccoli spears
Salt to taste

For the mornay sauce
2 tablespoons
  cornflour
450ml milk
50g fresh Parmesan,
  grated
50g Gruyère, grated
A knob of butter
Salt and pepper
  to taste

1. Either boil or steam the broccoli until tender. Drain and sprinkle with a little salt.

2. Put the broccoli in a buttered ovenproof dish.

3. To make the sauce, mix the cornflour in a jug with 4 tablespoons of the milk to make a smooth paste. Heat the rest of the milk in a saucepan.

4. When the milk is just beginning to boil, pour it into the flour and milk paste and whisk to combine.

5. Pour the sauce back into the pan and heat gently back to boiling point, stirring all the time. Lower the heat and simmer for 2 minutes. Remove from the heat, stir in the cheeses and butter and season to taste with salt and pepper.

6. Pour the sauce over the cooked broccoli and place under a hot grill until the top browns. Serve immediately.

Spicy Battered Hake with Parsnip Fries

180g plain flour
2 teaspoons mild
  curry powder
½ level teaspoon salt
1 teaspoon cumin seeds
1 teaspoon brown
  mustard seeds
2 eggs
1 tablespoon
  sunflower oil
150ml milk, or 100ml
  milk and 50ml water
  mixed together
Sufficient oil for
  frying the fish
4 × 150–175g
  hake fillets
3–4 parsnips, peeled
  and cut into
  fingers, dried well
  before frying

1. Sieve the flour, curry powder and salt into a bowl.

2. Stir in the seeds.

3. Make a well in the centre of the flour and add the eggs, oil and about 50ml of the milk (or milk and water mixture). Whisk until everything is blended together, then whisk in the rest of the milk gradually.

4. Heat the oil in a deep pan or fryer. Dip the fish into the batter and place each fillet carefully into the hot oil. Fry for about 4½ minutes until the batter is deep golden, then place the cooked fish on a piece of kitchen paper to absorb the excess oil.

5. When all the fish portions are cooked, put them on a plate to keep warm in the oven while you fry the parsnip fingers.

6. Sprinkle the parsnip fingers with a little salt and lower them carefully into the hot oil. Fry for about 4 minutes, depending on the thickness of the parsnips, and drain on a piece of kitchen paper.

7. Serve the fish and fries together on a plate with some mayonnaise or tartare sauce.

Rhubarb Crumble

Rhubarb crumble is a favourite in our home, and cooking the rhubarb in the oven with a little sugar adds to the flavour.

Serves 4 generous portions

8 sticks of rhubarb, cut into 4cm chunks
5 tablespoons golden caster sugar
2 tablespoons honey
180g plain flour
20g porridge oats
120g butter
100g soft brown sugar
1 level teaspoon ground ginger (optional)

1. Preheat the oven to 180°C/gas mark 4.

2. Put the rhubarb pieces in a bowl and sprinkle with a little water to moisten.

3. Arrange the rhubarb on a baking sheet, sprinkle with the sugar and drizzle with the honey. Bake in the preheated oven for about 10–12 minutes, or until just tender.

4. Meanwhile, make the topping by sieving the flour into a mixing bowl and stir in the porridge oats. Rub in the butter until the mixture looks like breadcrumbs and stir in the sugar.

5. When the rhubarb is cooked, sprinkle evenly with the ginger, if using.

6. Spoon the rhubarb into an ovenproof dish and spread the crumble mixture over the top.

7. Bake for 30–40 minutes until the top of the crumble is golden brown. Serve with freshly made custard, cream or ice cream.

Winter Vegetable Soup

This is a thick, hearty broth that contains pearl barley. For variety, add other vegetables that you've frozen, if you wish, such as peas or green beans.

Serves 6

1.5 litres chicken or
    vegetable stock
100g pearl barley
50g butter
2 leeks, sliced thinly
1 small onion, chopped
2 carrots, chopped
Half a small swede,
    chopped
2 parsnips, peeled
    and chopped
2 medium potatoes,
    peeled and diced
100g celeriac, chopped
2 bay leaves
1 teaspoon
    dried thyme
Salt and pepper
    to taste

1. Pour the stock into a large saucepan and add the barley. Bring to a simmer and continue to simmer gently for 15 minutes.

2. In another pan, melt the butter, then add the leeks and onion and allow them to sweat on a low heat for a few minutes. Add the carrots, swede and parsnips. Cover and cook very gently for about 10 minutes.

3. Add the potatoes, celeriac, bay leaves and thyme. Cover and simmer for 4 more minutes. Turn up the heat and add the stock and barley, stirring well.

4. Bring to the boil, then turn down the heat and simmer for 20 minutes, stirring occasionally. Check for seasoning; depending on how much salt was in the stock, you may only need to add pepper.

5. When the soup is cooked, either serve immediately or allow to cool, then reheat when necessary. If you do this, don't allow it to boil; just heat it slowly to simmering or the flavours will be impaired.

Storage suggestion
Any leftover soup may be stored in the fridge for up to 2 days in a covered container. Reheat as described before.

Smoked Mackerel Pâté

This is wonderful as a quick snack or a starter course.

Serves 4 generously

350–375g smoked
  mackerel
Ground black pepper
  to taste
150g low-fat
  cream cheese
Juice of half a lemon

1. Remove the skin and any bones from the fish and place the flesh in a bowl. Break up any large flakes and season with black pepper.

2. Add the cream cheese and lemon juice and beat together with a spatula or wooden spoon until it is as smooth as you wish.

3. Spoon into a serving dish or ramekins if you wish to serve individual portions.

Swede and Potato Bake

This combination tastes so savoury, especially with plenty of white pepper. It can be served on its own or with roast beef or pork, and it is simply sublime with sausages.

Serves 4

600g swede, diced
450g potatoes, diced
   slightly larger than
   the swede
50g butter
1 small onion, chopped
3 tablespoons
   single cream
A little grated nutmeg
Salt and pepper
   to taste
100g Cheddar, grated
50g fresh breadcrumbs,
   white or wholemeal

1. Boil the swede and potatoes in enough salted water just to cover them.

2. Melt 25g of the butter in a frying pan and fry the onions gently, without browning, until they are soft.

3. When the potatoes and swede are tender, drain well and put back in the pan. Add the rest of the butter, the cream and nutmeg and season to taste with salt and pepper. Mash well.

4. Preheat the oven to 200°C/gas mark 6. Butter an ovenproof dish.

5. Put the onions at the bottom of the dish and spoon the vegetable mash over the top, smoothing out the top with a fork.

6. Combine the cheese and breadcrumbs and sprinkle over the top.

7. Bake for about 20 minutes, or until the edges are golden brown. Serve immediately.

Duck Breasts with Orange and Ginger Sauce

You can also use goose breasts for this recipe. If you're not keen on the flavour of ginger, simply omit it – the dish tastes just as good without.

Serves 4

4 duck breast fillets

For the sauce
I teaspoon grated
   fresh ginger
150ml fresh
   orange juice
Zest of I orange
I tablespoon soft
   brown sugar
I tablespoon soy sauce
I tablespoon
   dry sherry
I tablespoon
   balsamic vinegar

1. Preheat the oven to 200°C/gas mark 6.

2. Put all the sauce ingredients into a bowl and whisk together.

3. Make small cuts in the duck flesh along the skin side of the breasts and place them, skin-side up, on a trivet in a roasting pan. Brush the skin with some of the prepared sauce and roast in the preheated oven for about 20 minutes.

4. Meanwhile, put the sauce in a small pan and bring to the boil. Boil for about 8 minutes, until it is reduced and begins to thicken.

5. When the duck breasts are cooked, allow them to rest for 5 minutes, then slice and put on a plate. Pour on the sauce and serve.

Serving suggestion
This goes really well with the stir-fried noodles on the next page.

Stir-fried Noodles

These noodles make a perfect partner to any stir-fry, and they only take a few minutes to prepare.

Serves 4

400g medium-sized
  noodles
1 tablespoon
  sesame oil
1 tablespoon
  sunflower oil
Half a small leek,
  cut into very
  thin strips
1 medium carrot,
  grated
1 garlic clove, grated
2 tablespoons
  soy sauce
2 tablespoons
  dry sherry
2 tablespoons honey

1. Boil the noodles until cooked, then drain well and leave in the pan.

2. In a wok or deep frying pan, heat the sesame and sunflower oils. Add the vegetables and fry for 2–3 minutes, stirring constantly.

3. Stir in the garlic.

4. Add the noodles and fry for 20–30 seconds, then add the soy sauce, sherry and honey and stir to coat the noodles and vegetables.

5. Serve immediately.

Rabbit in White Wine

This is a slow-cooked dish and can be left to 'do its thing', so it is very easy to prepare. Rabbit is a very lean meat, which is why bacon has been used to help it cook by adding a bit of fat.

Serves 4

30g butter
1 tablespoon oil
4 rashers of streaky
  bacon, chopped
1 jointed rabbit
1 large onion, chopped
2 carrots, sliced
  into discs
Salt and pepper
  to taste
¼ teaspoon dried
  thyme
180ml dry white wine
2 tablespoons
  Dijon mustard

1. Preheat the oven to 190°C/gas mark 5.

2. Melt the butter in a frying pan and heat it together with the oil. Fry the bacon until the fat runs and the meat starts to brown. Put the bacon into a lidded ovenproof casserole dish.

3. Put the rabbit portions into the fat and fry for 2–3 minutes. Add to the bacon.

4. Fry the onions in the same pan, then spoon them into the casserole.

5. Stir in the carrots, season with salt and pepper and add the thyme.

6. Add the wine to the pan along with the mustard and bring to the boil. Pour over the rabbit mixture.

7. Cover and place in the oven. Cook for 1¼ hours, or until the rabbit is tender.

Serving suggestion
Serve with creamed or boiled potatoes and green cabbage.

Broccoli and Cheese Tart

Serve this tart hot or cold, accompanied by the coleslaw on page 36.

Serves 4

250g shortcrust pastry
About 8 broccoli
   florets, steamed or
   boiled until tender
1 egg
50ml milk
100ml single cream
120g Cheddar or
   Stilton, grated
   or crumbled

1. Preheat the oven to 200°C/gas mark 6. Grease a 20cm flan tin.

2. Roll out the pastry to fit the tin with a little to spare and line the tin with it. Line the pastry with a circle of greaseproof paper about 6–7cm larger than the flan tin. Weigh down with baking beans or dried beans and bake for 10 minutes. Remove the beans and paper.

3. Arrange the broccoli evenly over the pastry and sprinkle with the cheese.

4. Mix the egg, milk and cream together and pour over the filling.

5. Cook the tart for about 30 minutes until the filling is set and the top has turned golden in colour.

6. Cool for 5 minutes before serving, or serve cold.

Coleslaw

Coleslaw goes very well with savoury tarts or pizzas – and with fried chicken, too.

Serves 4

Half a small onion,
  white or red
1 medium carrot,
  grated
¼ shredded white, red
  or the inner part of
  a green cabbage
3 rounded tablespoons
  good mayonnaise

1. Chop the onion finely and mix it into the grated carrot.

2. Shred the cabbage as finely as you prefer and mix that into the carrot and onion.

3. Add the mayonnaise and stir well to combine.

4. Transfer to a serving dish and serve.

Variation
Try mixing in some chopped fresh parsley with the other ingredients.

Lemon Sole Nutty Rolls

An unusual way to cook lemon sole. These rolls can be served with any seasonal green vegetable.

Serves 4

100g fresh
 breadcrumbs
50g chopped hazelnuts
25g ground almonds
Juice of 1 lemon
2 tablespoons fresh
 chopped parsley
2 small eggs, beaten
Salt and pepper
 to taste
4 lemon sole fillets
8 thin rashers
 streaky bacon

1. Preheat the oven to 180°C/gas mark 4.

2. In a large bowl, mix the breadcrumbs, nuts, lemon juice, parsley and enough eggs to form a soft but not runny mixture. Season with salt and pepper to taste. Mix thoroughly.

3. Spread a quarter of the filling mixture over the surface of the fish.

4. Flatten 2 rashers of bacon and overlap them by about 1cm.

5. Roll up one fish fillet, taking care not to lose much filling. Put the fillet on the flattened bacon strips close to one end and roll the bacon around the fish. Repeat with the other three fillets and the rest of the bacon.

6. Place in a lightly buttered baking dish or roasting tin. Cover with foil and bake for 20–25 minutes. Remove the foil for the last 10 minutes.

7. Serve with mashed potatoes and tartare sauce.

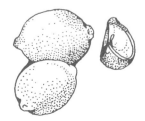

Beekeeper's Casserole

Just why this has been given such a specific name is unknown, except for the fact that it contains honey. Whatever its origins, it is a tasty vegetable dish that's good on its own with bread, or served as an accompaniment with cooked ham or roasted meats.

Serves 6 as an accompaniment or 4 as a main meal

1 cabbage weighing
  600–675g
1 large apple (any kind
  will do)
1 onion, chopped
1 medium parsnip,
  peeled and diced
2 large potatoes,
  peeled and diced
3 tablespoons
  white-wine vinegar
2 tablespoons honey
Salt and pepper
  to taste
30g butter
4 tablespoons water

1. Preheat the oven to 150°C/gas mark 2.

2. Shred the cabbage, removing the thick stalks, and place it in a bowl.

3. Add the apple, onion, parsnip and potatoes and combine with your hands.

4. Whisk the vinegar and honey together and season to taste with salt and pepper.

5. Melt the butter in a pan. Place the vegetable mixture in a buttered ovenproof dish and drizzle it with the vinegar mixture, then the water.

6. Pour the melted butter over the vegetables, cover with a lid or foil and place in the oven for 1 hour. Lift out and stir, then cover and cook for about 30 more minutes.

Kale and Potato Omelette

One of the most delicious Spanish omelettes is made very simply, with potato, onion and eggs. Adding seasonal vegetables throughout the year simply builds on a good thing!

Serves 2–3

2 tablespoons olive oil
1 small onion, chopped
2 medium potatoes,
  peeled and diced
400g kale, shredded
  and chopped
Salt and pepper
  to taste
6 eggs, beaten

1. Heat the oil gently in a deep frying pan and add the onion. Fry gently for 3–4 minutes, or until soft.

2. While the onion cooks, boil the potatoes in salted water for 3 minutes.

3. Once the onion is soft, add the kale and potatoes and fry everything together for 3 minutes. Season with salt and pepper.

4. Add the eggs and cook until they set. If the top is still runny, place the pan under a hot grill to set the top. Serve in wedges with bread.

Variation
Sprinkle the top with your favourite cheese before grilling.

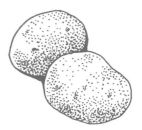

Three Cheese and Leek Pie

This makes a real change from an ordinary cheese and onion pie.

Serves 4–6

15g butter
2 medium leeks,
    chopped
300g shortcrust pastry
100g mature
    Cheddar, grated
120g red Leicester,
    cubed
120g Cheshire,
    Lancashire or other
    crumbly cheese
1 egg
White pepper
    to taste

1. Preheat the oven to 200°C/gas mark 6. Grease a deep 20cm pie plate or dish.

2. Heat the butter in a frying pan and fry the leeks until just soft.

3. Roll out two-thirds of the pastry and line the pie dish with it. Don't trim off any edges yet.

4. Sprinkle the grated Cheddar over the bottom of the pastry. Add the cooked leeks.

5. Spread the cubed Red Leicester over the filling and crumble over the other cheese.

6. Beat the egg and pour over the cheese. Give it a quick stir to make sure everything is evenly combined. Season with pepper.

7. Roll out the other third of the pastry to use as the the pie lid. Moisten the edges around the pie and fit the lid. Crimp around the edge to seal.

8. Bake for 35–40 minutes, or until the pastry is golden brown. Serve hot or cold.

Pancakes with Lemon Sauce

Pancake day is tradition in most households, although pancakes are eaten on many other days as well. The British version usually serves them with lemon and sugar, honey or syrup, but try this lemony, buttery sauce for a change – it's also delicious served with hot sponge puddings and ice cream.

Serves 4

For the pancakes
120g plain flour
A pinch of salt
2 eggs, beaten
280ml milk
Oil or melted butter
 for frying

For the sauce
100g caster sugar
2 level teaspoons
 of cornflour mixed
 with 3 teaspoons
 of water to form
 a smooth paste
Juice and zest of
 1 lemon
80ml water
50g butter

1. Sieve the flour into a bowl with the salt and make a well in the centre.

2. Add the eggs and whisk them into the flour together with about 2 tablespoons of the milk.

3. When the eggs and flour are fully mixed, whisk in the milk, about 50ml at a time.

4. Heat a small, pancake-sized frying pan with a few drops of oil or melted butter and add about 2 tablespoons of the batter, swirling the pan so that the pancake is even. Fry for about 30 seconds, then turn over and fry for about 20 seconds.

5. Use a spatula and transfer the pancake to a plate in a warm oven. Continue cooking the pancakes and place a piece of greaseproof paper between each so that they don't stick together.

For the sauce
1. Put all the ingredients except the butter in a pan over a gentle heat and stir until the mixture simmers.

2. Add the butter and beat until it thickens. Remove from the heat. Serve hot or cold.

Dried-fruit Compote with Brandy

This makes an excellent fruit dessert when fresh fruit has become less seasonal. The brandy may be omitted if necessary, but it makes for an excellent special-occasion pudding course.

Serves 6

600g mixed dried fruit:
  prunes, apples,
  apricots, pears,
  peaches, etc.
100ml apple juice
100ml fresh
  orange juice
50ml water
2 tablespoons soft
  brown sugar
½ teaspoon
  vanilla extract
3 tablespoons brandy

For the
Chantilly cream
280ml double cream
1 rounded tablespoon
  icing sugar
1 teaspoon
  vanilla extract

1. Put all the fruit into a pan along with the juices, water and sugar. Bring to the boil, then simmer for 10 minutes.

2. Add the vanilla and the brandy and simmer for 2 more minutes.

3. Remove from the heat and serve with Chantilly cream or double cream.

For the Chantilly cream
Whisk all the ingredients together lightly until fluffy but not stiff.

Farmhouse Fruit Cake

Dried fruit is so useful and makes a delicious and satisfying cake, especially at this time of the year when you sometimes need a cake treat to comfort you during a cold spell.

Makes 8–10 portions

180g butter
180g golden
   caster sugar
220g self-raising flour
2 medium eggs
½ level teaspoon
   cinnamon
A pinch nutmeg
Zest of 1 lemon
25g currants
50g raisins
25g sultanas
4 tablespoons milk
1 dessertspoon
   demerara sugar,
   for sprinkling

1. Grease and line an 18cm round cake tin. Preheat the oven to 180°C/gas mark 4.

2. Cream the butter and sugar together until very light and fluffy.

3. Add a tablespoon of the flour and beat in the eggs.

4. Sieve the flour and spices together into the creamed mixture and begin to fold in.

5. Add the lemon zest and dried fruit and finish folding in.

6. Stir in the milk, then spoon the mixture into the prepared tin. Sprinkle a little sugar over the top for a crispy topping.

7. Bake for 1–1¼ hours until deep golden in colour. Cool before serving.

Dried Apricot Jam

This wonderful preserve makes tasty jam tarts and is also good with scones as a change from your usual jam. Omit the almonds if you prefer, but they do go well with the flavour of the apricots.

Makes 4 x 450g jars

500g dried apricots
Water to soak the apricots: enough to cover by 2cm
Juice of 1 lemon
1.5kg sugar
50g flaked almonds

1. Put the apricots into a bowl and pour over hot (not boiling) water. Leave to soak for 6–8 hours or overnight.

2. Place the fruit and the liquid in a large pan. Add the lemon juice and bring to the boil, then simmer for 25 minutes, or until the apricots are very tender. Remove from the heat and turn the heat down.

3. Stir in the sugar and almonds and return to a low heat, stirring until the sugar has dissolved.

4. Turn the heat up and bring to the boil. Boil for 5–6 minutes, then test for a setting point (see page 19).

5. Pot immediately and label. This will store unopened for about 12–18 months. If you want to make a bigger batch of jam, simply double the quantities.

Pickled Red Cabbage

Pickling fresh vegetables is a lot easier than you think. This is a must for serving with hotpots and potato pie.

Makes 5 x 450g jars

1 large red cabbage
About 1 litre
   spiced vinegar
   (see page 23)
Salt

1. Shred the cabbage and layer it in a dish, sprinkling each layer liberally with salt. Leave for 24 hours.

2. Rinse the cabbage thoroughly and pack into sterilised jars, covering it with the vinegar. Seal immediately.

3. This is ready to eat after 5 days. Use within 3 months or 2 weeks when opened. Best stored in the fridge after opening.

Variation
White cabbage may be prepared in the same way, but it will keep for 2 months.

Once springtime is finally on its way, there is a different feel about the mornings, and the trees are ready to burst into life. Yet it can still be cold and frosty, so sustaining and cheering puddings and cakes are still definitely on the menu. Lamb is traditionally associated with this time of year, and it is usually enjoyed with fresh-tasting mint.

March is the time when most seeds are sown in millions of furrows in gardens, allotments and fields around the country. Imperceptibly, the soil starts to warm, and despite the odd peppering of snow, crops benefit from it. By the end of the month the temperature will have risen by five degrees, and this will double plant metabolism. March is also the time when the sun is strong enough to force plants to store sugar, so all our food is getting sweeter from this point on.

Easter very rarely falls in March, but the dish known as Easter ledger is readily available. The plant that makes it is bistort, and this bitter pudding was once eaten in silence by devout Christians. As March becomes full-blown spring, oxalic acid builds up in the bistort leaves, just as it does in many spring vegetables, and it becomes more and more difficult to eat – and even harder to digest.

Salmon is the biggest March treat, particularly if you've been lucky enough to catch one yourself. Salmon and cockles make a special treat: simply bake salmon with a white wine and cream sauce to go with the cockles for a real taste of the seaside.

March

March Menu

A three-course meal to serve 4 people

✻

Salmon Parcels with Sorrel Sauce

✻

Spring Lamb with Fresh Mint Sauce

✻

Marmalade Roly Poly

Salmon Parcels with Sorrel Sauce

Cooking the salmon in a baking-paper parcel keeps all the flavour locked in the fish. This is a very easy dish to serve as a starter.

4 salmon fillets, each
weighing about 100g
A squeeze of lemon
for each fillet
Salt and pepper
to taste
4 teaspoons olive oil

For the sauce
25g butter
2 shallots
1 bunch sorrel leaves:
about 20, thick stalks
removed, chopped
roughly, plus extra
for sprinkling
80ml dry white wine
Salt and pepper
to taste
100ml double cream

1. Preheat the oven to 190°C/gas mark 5.

2. Put each salmon fillet in the centre of a piece of baking parchment big enough to fold into a parcel securely. Squeeze about a teaspoon of lemon juice over each fillet and season with salt and pepper. Drizzle the olive oil evenly over each.

3. Fold the edges of the parchment together and fold down the join – like making a paper fan but folding in the same direction. Tuck the ends under the parcel and place on a baking sheet. Bake for 15 minutes.

4. While the fish cooks, make the sauce. Melt the butter in a pan over a fairly low heat and add the shallots. Fry gently until they are translucent.

5. Add the sorrel and wine and cook for 3 minutes. Season with salt and pepper.

6. Add the cream and remove from the heat.

7. When the salmon has finished cooking, put each fillet on a plate and spoon the sauce on top. Add a sprinkling of chopped fresh sorrel leaves to serve.

Spring Lamb with Fresh Mint Sauce

You can do so many sauces and add a variety of ingredients to lamb, but to really bring out its best, nothing beats mint. Lamb is so sweet-tasting that the tang of mint complements it better than any other flavour. If you make more sauce than you need, it will keep for six to eight weeks in a sterilised screwtop jar.

Serves 4

12 lamb cutlets, excess
    fat removed
A little oil, for roasting
Salt and pepper
    to taste

For the sauce
50g mint leaves
A pinch of salt
150ml white vinegar
25g soft brown sugar
50ml boiling water

First, make the sauce

1. To make the sauce, finely chop the mint leaves and put them into a glass bowl. Sprinkle with a little salt and pour over the vinegar.

2. Stir the sugar into the boiling water and dissolve it completely, then pour this over the mint and vinegar. Allow to marinate for 2 hours before using.

Now, cook the cutlets

3. Preheat the oven to 200°C/gas mark 6.

4. Brush the cutlets with a little oil. Season with salt and pepper.

5. Place in a roasting tin and roast for about 15–20 minutes, depending on how you like them cooked.

6. Serve the cutlets with the mint sauce.

Serving suggestion
This goes well with fried cubed potatoes and steamed or boiled green cabbage served with a knob of butter.

MINT

Marmalade Roly Poly

Use Old English Marmalade for this if you can. It tastes wonderful!

Serves 4 generously

Marmalade

For the pastry
200g self-raising flour
A pinch of salt
100g vegetarian suet
Water: enough to mix
to a soft dough

To make the pastry
1. Sieve the flour and salt together into a bowl and stir in the suet.

2. Add 2 tablespoons water and stir in. Continue adding a little water at a time until you have a soft dough you'll be able to roll out lightly.

3. Use your hands to gather the mixture into a ball.

4. Knead very lightly until smooth.

To make the roly-poly
1. Preheat the oven to 200°C/gas mark 6.

2. Roll out the pastry to about 4mm thick and 25cm square.

3. Spread with sufficient marmalade to cover the surface of the pastry. Leave the edges clear, however, or it will ooze out.

4. Dampen the edges and roll up.

5. Place on a greased baking sheet and bake for 30–40 minutes. Serve hot with custard.

Broccoli and Potato Soup

This is a delicious combination of flavours and makes a substantial lunch or supper dish. Even those who aren't keen on broccoli as a vegetable like this soup.

Serves 4

25g butter
1 onion, finely chopped
4 rashers unsmoked
  bacon, chopped
1 garlic clove, grated
400g broccoli spears,
  chopped roughly
300g potatoes,
  peeled and diced
1 litre vegetable or
  chicken stock
Salt and pepper
  to taste
100ml single cream

1. Melt the butter in a large pan over a low heat and fry the onion until soft.

2. Add the bacon and garlic and fry until the bacon has cooked.

3. Add the broccoli and potatoes and heat for a few minutes, stirring gently.

4. Pour in the stock and turn up the heat. Bring to the boil and season to taste.

5. Turn the heat down to simmering and cook until the vegetables are tender – about 20 minutes.

6. Remove from the heat and liquidise – or use a hand blender to achieve the texture of your choice.

7. Return to the heat. Add the cream and stir until the soup bubbles gently. Serve immediately.

Serving suggestion
Try sprinkling a little crumbly Lancashire or Wensleydale cheese on the top before serving.

Dandelion and Nettle Soup

An unusual soup, but one that still tastes delicious. When you pick the nettles don't forget to wear gloves and only pick the new tops of the plant. The same goes for dandelion leaves: in spring they are mostly new leaves, but pick only the newest and smallest leaves. Make sure you pick from a place where they haven't been previously sprayed with weedkiller. Wash the leaves thoroughly before use. For absolute safety, cultivate dandelions in your garden for kitchen use.

Serves 2–3

30g butter
1 large onion,
    finely chopped
2 medium carrots,
    diced
2 medium potatoes,
    peeled and diced
1 garlic clove, grated
100g nettle tops
100g young
    dandelion leaves
1 bay leaf
2 sprigs fresh thyme
700ml vegetable or
    chicken stock
½ teaspoon celery salt
Pepper to taste

1. Melt the butter in a saucepan and sauté the onions and carrots for 3 minutes.

2. Add the potatoes and sauté for 2 more minutes.

3. Stir in the garlic and the nettles and dandelion leaves.

4. Add the bay leaf and thyme and pour in the stock. Add the celery salt and pepper. Bring to the boil, then turn down the heat and simmer for 25–30 minutes.

5. Remove the bay leaf and liquidise the soup. Reheat if necessary before serving.

Lemon Couscous

This makes a good salad base in the summer months, with chopped tomato, cucumber and red pepper added. To add even more flavour, mix the boiling water with a good-quality vegetable stock cube before pouring over the couscous.

Serves 4

200g couscous
Boiling water:
    enough to cover
    the couscous
½ teaspoon salt
2 teaspoons olive oil
Juice and zest of
    1 lemon

1. Put the couscous in a large bowl and pour over sufficient boiling water to cover it with about 2cm to spare.

2. Stir in the salt, oil and lemon zest and juice.

3. Cover and leave for about 5 minutes until all the liquid has been absorbed.

Serving suggestion
This goes very well with the baked mackerel on p54.

Baked Mackerel with Apple Stuffing

Oily fish are so good for you. They don't need much in the way of added flavours, but this stuffing mixture of apple and onion goes so well with the meaty flesh of the fish that it would be a shame not to try it.

Serves 4

Half a lemon
4 prepared mackerel
50g butter
I small onion, chopped
   very finely
2 smallish apples,
   peeled, cored
   and diced
200g fresh white
   breadcrumbs
I egg, beaten
3 tablespoons flour
   seasoned with a
   little salt and pepper

1. Rub the lemon over the mackerel, inside and out.

2. Melt a knob of the butter in a pan and fry the onion gently until tender.

3. Add the apple to the onions and cook for 2 minutes.

4. Put the breadcrumbs in a bowl and pour over the onion and apple mixture. Stir well.

5. Melt the rest of the butter in the same pan and stir into the breadcrumb mixture.

6. Preheat the oven to 190°C/gas mark 5.

7. Dip the mackerel first in the egg, then in the seasoned flour and sprinkle a little in the inside of each fish.

8. Stuff each fish with a quarter of the stuffing and lay them in an oiled roasting tin or ovenproof dish.

9. Bake the mackerel for 25–30 minutes. Serve with lemon couscous (see page 53).

Pigeon Pie

A rich-tasting pie that contains beef as well as pigeon. The meat content of the bird itself is quite small, but it is nonetheless rich in flavour.

Serves 4

5 prepared pigeons
Water: enough to
    make the stock
300g best braising
    steak, cut into
    small chunks
25g freshly
    chopped parsley
½ teaspoon
    dried thyme
Salt and pepper
    to taste
2 teaspoons cornflour
    (optional)
250g shortcrust pastry

1. Keep the breast meat to one side in a cool place and put the rest of the pigeon carcasses in sufficient water to cover. Bring to the boil, then simmer for 1½ hours. This will be the stock for the gravy.

2. Preheat the oven to 180°C/gas mark 4.

3. Butter a deep pie dish and place the braising steak chunks in the bottom.

4. Cut each pigeon breast in half and lay the pieces on top of the beef.

5. Sprinkle the herbs over the meat and season well with salt and pepper.

6. Pour in enough prepared pigeon stock to cover the meat by 2cm.

7. Cover with foil and stand the dish on a baking sheet. Place in the oven and cook for 1½ hours.

8. Remove the dish from the oven and raise the heat to 200°C/gas mark 6.

9. Thicken the gravy if you wish with 2 teaspoons of cornflour mixed with a little cold water to make a thin paste. Stir well into the gravy.

10. Roll out the pastry to fit the top of the dish and cut a slit in the centre to allow steam to escape. Bake for 30 minutes, or until the pastry is golden.

Serving suggestion
Serve with crispy homemade chips to dip into the gorgeous gravy.

Sea Bass with a Rocket and Butter Sauce

The peppery taste of rocket goes beautifully with the firm, subtly flavoured flesh of the fish.

Serves 4

4 sea bass fillets
Salt and pepper
   to taste
Oil for frying

For the sauce
50g butter
3 anchovies
2 or 3 shallots,
   depending on size,
   chopped finely
250ml vegetable or
   fish stock
200g rocket,
   roughly chopped
50ml single cream

First, make the sauce
1. Melt the butter in a small pan and add the anchovies. Stir them into the butter until they have almost dissolved.

2. Add the shallots and fry gently for a few minutes until tender.

3. Add the stock and bring to the boil.

4. Add the rocket to the sauce. Turn down the heat and simmer for 3–4 minutes.

5. Purèe the sauce in a blender or with a hand blender, then reheat it to simmering and stir in the cream.

Now cook the fish
1. Season the fish with a little salt and pepper. Fry on a medium heat in about 3 tablespoons of oil for 3–4 minutes on each side, depending on size.

2. Reheat the sauce if necessary before serving. Serve with mashed potatoes.

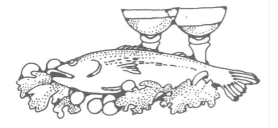

Stir-fry Chicken and Spring Onions in Hoi Sin Sauce

A quick and tasty dish that is good with noodles.

Serves 4

1 tablespoon
   sesame oil
1 tablespoon
   sunflower oil
2 garlic cloves, chopped
450g chicken breasts,
   cut into small,
   thin strips
8 spring onions, sliced
   into thin strips
2 dark-green
   cabbage leaves,
   shredded finely
3 tablespoons
   dry sherry
2 tablespoons
   soy sauce
4 tablespoons hoi sin
   sauce mixed with
   2 tablespoons water

1. Heat a wok or large frying pan and add the oils and garlic. Stir-fry for a few seconds on a high heat.

2. Add the chicken and fry until it changes colour all over.

3. Add the spring onions and fry for 1 minute. Add the cabbage and sherry, soy and hoi sin sauce. Fry everything together for 2 minutes.

4. Serve with egg noodles.

Wensleydale and Red Onion Marmalade Tart

To go with this tart, you can use red onion marmalade that you made last autumn, or try this quick recipe for a small fresh batch.

For the marmalade

1 large red onion or
    8 young red onions,
    chopped very finely
2 tablespoons soft
    brown sugar
2 tablespoons
    white-wine vinegar
Pinch of salt

For the tart

250g shortcrust pastry
4–5 tablespoons red
    onion marmalade
250g Wensleydale
    cheese, crumbled
    or chopped rather
    than grated
1 small egg
75ml single cream
Black pepper to taste

For the marmalade

1. Put all the ingredients in a pan and heat gently until the sugar has dissolved.

2. Bring to the boil, then turn down the heat and simmer gently for 35–40 minutes until thick and glossy. Stir occasionally.

3. Allow to cool thoroughly before using in the tart.

For the tart

1. Preheat the oven to 200°C/gas mark 6. Grease a 20cm flan tin.

2. Roll out the pastry to fit the tin with a little to spare and line the tin with it.

3. Line the pastry with a circle of greaseproof paper about 6–7cm bigger than the tin. Weigh down with baking beans or dried beans and bake for 10 minutes. Remove the beans and paper.

4. Spoon the marmalade over the pastry base and spread it out evenly.

5. Sprinkle the cheese over the marmalade and press it down lightly so that the cheese and marmalade combine.

6. Beat the egg and the cream together and pour over the tart.

7. Season with black pepper to taste and bake the tart for 25–30 minutes.

Serving suggestion
Serve with baby salad leaves: a combination of beet, rocket, lettuce, dandelion, sorrel and endive or whatever you have growing. Dress the leaves with a little balsamic vinegar.

Grilled Sardines with Tomato Sauce

Sardines make a very quick supper dish and go so well with this tangy tomato sauce. Serve with crusty bread and salad leaves.

Serves 4

12–16 sardines
A little salt and pepper
  to taste

For the sauce
2 tablespoons olive oil
1 small onion, very
  finely chopped
1 garlic clove, chopped
200ml passata
½ teaspoon salt
2 teaspoons
  brown sugar
2 tablespoons
  balsamic vinegar

1. Preheat the grill to hot.

2. Begin the sauce by heating the oil in a saucepan and frying the onions and garlic gently until soft. While the onions are softening, place the sardines on an oiled baking sheet and season with salt and pepper. Put them under the grill.

3. Add the passata and other ingredients to the onions and simmer gently, stirring constantly, for 2 minutes, or until the sugar has dissolved.

4. When the sardines have been cooking for about 4 minutes, turn them over and cook for a further 4 minutes on the other side.

5. By the time the fish are cooked, the sauce will be ready to serve.

Simnel Cake

Early March is the best time to make this traditional Easter cake, although it is a good excuse to make a rich fruit cake when you have run out of Christmas cake. This recipe is best eaten four weeks after being made, because the flavours will have developed and matured. It is an almond paste-lover's dream as it contains a layer in the centre as well as one on top.

Serves 8–10

For the almond paste
120g caster sugar
120g ground almonds
1 egg
½ teaspoon
   almond extract

For the cake
120g butter
120g soft brown sugar
160g plain flour
3 eggs, beaten
½ teaspoon
   mixed spice
350g mixed dried
   fruit: raisins, sultanas
   and currants
Zest and juice of
   1 lemon

Apricot jam or
   marmalade,
   for the top

For the almond paste
1. In a bowl combine the sugar and ground almonds.

2. Beat the egg and add enough of the dry ingredients to it to make a soft, pliable dough.

3. Knead in the almond extract until well mixed. Cover and leave to one side.

For the cake
1. Preheat the oven to 140°C/gas mark 1. Grease and line a deep 18cm cake tin.

2. Cream the butter and sugar until light and fluffy.

3. Add a tablespoon of the flour and gradually beat in the eggs.

4. Sift the flour and spice together. Sprinkle a tablespoon over the dried fruit and mix well, then add the rest of the sifted flour to the creamed mixture.

5. Fold in the flour and add the fruit as you fold so it all combines well. As you add the fruit, pour in the lemon juice and zest. Mix well but gently.

6. Spoon half the cake mixture into the tin. Smooth it out with the back of the spoon to make a flat top.

7. Roll out a third of the almond paste to fit exactly over the cake mixture.

8. Add the rest of the mixture to the tin over the almond paste and smooth out the top. Hollow out the centre so that the top of the cake cooks flat. Bake for 1¾ hours.

9. Test to see if it is cooked by pushing a metal skewer through the centre: it should have no mixture on it if it is ready. If it does, bake for 15 more minutes.

10. Cool for 15 minutes in the tin, then transfer to a wire rack.

11. When cool, brush the top with apricot jam or marmalade ready to take the almond paste covering.

12. Using the same amount of almond paste as before, roll out a disc to just fit the top and place it carefully onto the cake. Press down around the edges.

13. Roll the rest of the almond paste into 11 little balls and place them on a baking sheet. Put in the oven at 180°C/gas mark 4 for about 10 minutes, until they are golden brown.

14. Place the balls of almond paste around the outside edge of the cake. Wrap the cake in greaseproof paper and store it in an airtight tin for at least 2 weeks (but no more than 4).

Rhubarb Fool

Rhubarb is such a useful ingredient during the late winter and early spring, and it is versatile as well. This is one of the lighter desserts that you can make with it.

Serves 4

4 sticks rhubarb, cut
   into 2cm pieces
2 tablespoons water
75g soft brown sugar
120ml double cream
100ml natural
   low-fat yogurt
½ teaspoon
   vanilla extract
4 pieces of
   dark chocolate

1. Put the rhubarb into a sturdy pan over a low heat. Add the water and sugar and stir until the sugar has dissolved. Turn up the heat and simmer for about 10 minutes, or until the rhubarb is soft. Stir a few times during cooking. Allow to cool.

2. Put the cream and yogurt in a bowl. Add the vanilla and whisk until light and fluffy but not stiff.

3. Fold the cooled rhubarb and juice into the cream mixture. Don't mix it in fully as it is more interesting to eat when it is in separate places.

4. Spoon the mixture into large wine glasses.

5. Chill in the fridge for an hour before serving.

6. Grate or chop the dark chocolate and sprinkle it on top of the fool just before serving.

Rhubarb Jam

This will keep for a year unopened.

**Makes about
8 x 450g jars**

2kg rhubarb, cut into
   1.5cm pieces
2kg sugar
2cm piece root
   ginger, grated
4 tablespoons
   lemon juice
Knob of butter

1. Put the rhubarb into a large bowl and add the sugar. Cover and leave overnight.

2. Put the rhubarb and sugar in a large preserve-making pan over a low heat. Heat slowly, stirring in the ginger and lemon juice. Allow the sugar to dissolve fully before boiling.

3. Bring to the boil and continue to boil for 8–10 minutes, or until the rhubarb has sunk to the bottom of the pan. Test for setting point using a cold saucer (see page 19). Drop a small amount of the jam onto the saucer and push with your finger: it should wrinkle if ready.

4. Pot into sterilised jars, label and date.

April is a time to enjoy making good food. If you're lucky enough to be in the area, the walk from the wooded hills of east Anglesey to the ancient estuary at Aberffraw provides the hungry traveller with a stupendous meal. This month, the woodland floor is awash with amazing morel mushrooms. These fishnet-shaped fungi are wonderfully flavoured, but their aroma is one of the highlights of the season.

Along the sand dunes, the best rabbits from a warren that predates the Norman Conquest can be had – if you know the right youths and have a couple of quid to spare.

The river that drains the wooded marshes is home to the most stupendous watercress in Wales, and walking to the sea a mile away provides samphire and crab. This is the best salad in the world, and it fed the old king of Gwynedd, just as it still does any of his modern countrymen fortunate enough to know about it. Dandelion, nettle and sorrel are at their best here in April, and can also make 'Druid soup' – without the magical oaths, incantations and human sacrifice, of course. A word of warning, however: nettles grow where animals have urinated and they are none the worse for that, but felines urinate where dandelions grow, so you do need to be sure your supply is pee-free.

In Victorian times people grew dandelions in their gardens. The leaves were eaten when young and succulent, and they were smoked when old and hoary. Even as recently as 30 years ago some of the older generation of this country cured dandelion leaves to make their 'baccy' go further.

April

April Menu

A three-course meal to serve 4 people

~~

Crab and Salsify Cakes with Quick Lemon Mayonnaise

~~

Wood Pigeon with Morels and Sherry

~~

Banana Creams

Crab and Salsify Cakes with Quick Lemon Mayonnaise

The mayonnaise is very easy to make if you have a hand blender, and it goes really well with the crab cakes. If you can't find any salsify, substitute some finely chopped green beans or radish leaves.

100g salsify
2 teaspoons
    lemon juice
Salt and pepper
    to taste
250g potatoes, peeled,
    cut into small chunks
400g crabmeat
1 tablespoon chopped
    fresh parsley
1 egg yolk
Juice of half a lemon
4 tablespoons plain flour
About 4 tablespoons
    sunflower or
    vegetable oil,
    for frying

**For the lemon
mayonnaise**
4 egg yolks
½ teaspoon
    English mustard
Juice of 1 lemon
Pinch salt and pepper
    to taste
330ml light olive oil
    or sunflower oil

1. Cut the salsify into julienne strips and put them straight into enough cold water, mixed with 2 teaspoons of lemon juice, just to cover. Put the salsify and the lemon water they are in into a pan and bring to the boil. Add a pinch of salt. Boil for 5 minutes, or until tender. Drain.

2. In another saucepan, boil the potatoes until tender. Drain well and mash until smooth.

3. Put the crabmeat in a bowl and add the mashed potatoes, salsify and parsley and season with salt. Mix well with your hands.

4. Add the egg yolk and lemon juice. Mix into the other ingredients.

5. Form into patties whatever size you wish to serve and coat each in the flour.

6. Heat the oil in a frying pan and cook 4 patties at a time. Fry them for 3 minutes each side, then drain on kitchen paper.

7. Serve with some small lettuce leaves and the mayonnaise.

For the lemon mayonnaise
Put all the ingredients in a jug and use a hand blender to blend for about 40 seconds, or until creamy and fluffy. If you don't have a hand blender, whisk everything except the oil together, then add the oil in dribbles until it is all incorporated.

Wood Pigeon with Morels and Sherry

Wood pigeon may be bought at selected farmers' markets, or go on a shoot and bag your own. Any pigeon will do for this recipe, however, and the mushrooms go well with the meat's rich flavour.

30g butter
4 pigeons, dressed
50ml dry sherry
350ml chicken or
  vegetable stock
5 dried morel
  mushrooms
1 small onion,
  finely chopped
1 small stick celery,
  finely chopped
1 small carrot, cut into
  very small dice
50g button
  mushrooms, halved
1 teaspoon fresh
  thyme leaves
Salt and pepper
  to taste

1. Preheat the oven to 180°C/gas mark 4.

2. Melt half the butter in a frying pan over a medium heat and brown the pigeons. Put them into an ovenproof casserole dish.

3. Pour the sherry into the frying pan to deglaze it, then pour this liquid over the pigeon.

4. Heat the stock in a saucepan until hot and add the morels.

5. Put the rest of the butter in a frying pan and fry the onion, celery and carrot for 3–4 minutes. Add the button mushrooms and pour the vegetables over the pigeon. Sprinkle the thyme evenly over the dish.

6. Pour the stock and morels over the pigeon and cover.

7. Cook in the oven for about 30 minutes.

Serving suggestion
Serve with thinly cut chips or creamed potatoes.

Banana Creams

A quick and easy dessert for a dinner party that can be made beforehand.

2 level tablespoons
  cornflour mixed
  with 2 tablespoons
  water to make a
  smooth paste
250ml condensed milk
200ml single cream
3 egg yolks
1 teaspoon
  vanilla extract
20g butter
2 medium bananas
Juice of half a lemon

1. Put the cornflour mixture, condensed milk, cream and egg yolks in a pan and heat gently until the mixture simmers, stirring constantly. When it thickens, remove from the heat and whisk in the vanilla and butter. Allow to cool.

2. Peel the bananas and slice them into discs. Squeeze the lemon juice over them to prevent them from browning.

3. Arrange half of each banana in an individual soufflé-type dish and spoon the custard mixture over the top. Smooth out the top if necessary.

4. Chill for 1½ hours before serving.

Potted Shrimp or Prawns

You can buy brown shrimp from fish markets, but if you can't get hold of them use fresh or defrosted and drained prawns. This also makes an excellent sauce for topping baked white fish.

Serves 2–3

250g brown shrimp
  or prawns
Salt and black pepper
  to taste
80g melted butter
¼ teaspoon
  cayenne pepper

1. Force as many prawns or shrimp as will fit into ramekin dishes and season with salt and black pepper.

2. While the butter is melting, add the cayenne pepper and stir to mix thoroughly.

3. Pour the butter over the shrimp or prawns and allow to set before serving with hot toast. The butter from the prawns will melt into your toast.

Chervil Soufflé Omelette

This makes a quick lunch or supper dish served with a salad. If you have your own chickens and grow the chervil in your garden or in a pot, then the only cost to make this dish is the butter.

Serves 2

6 fresh eggs, separated
Pinch of salt
30g butter
4 stems of chervil,
    roughly chopped

1. Whisk the egg whites with a pinch of salt until fluffy but not too stiff.

2. Break up the yolks with a fork and fold into the whites.

3. Melt the butter in a frying pan and pour the egg mixture into the hot butter.

4. Sprinkle the chervil over the top and fry on a medium heat for about 4 minutes. The omelette won't set completely on the top, but you can put the pan under a grill briefly if you like a firmer omelette.

5. To serve, fold it in half in the pan, then cut in half and serve with bread and butter.

Spring Vegetable Soup

A light soup, but on a chilly spring day it will be very satisfying, especially when served with some brown or wholemeal bread.

Serves 6

50g butter
100g broccoli, chopped
5 large spring onions,
   finely chopped
2 leeks, chopped
3 medium green
   cabbage leaves,
   shredded
2 small carrots,
   chopped
1 tablespoon chopped
   fresh parsley
1 teaspoon fresh
   thyme leaves
1 bay leaf
1.2 litres water
   or vegetable stock
20g spinach leaves
20g rocket leaves,
   roughly chopped
Salt and pepper
   to taste

1. Melt the butter in a large lidded saucepan and add the broccoli, spring onions, leeks, cabbage, carrots and the herbs. Stir well so that everything is coated in the butter. Put on the lid and allow the vegetables to sweat over a very low heat for 12–15 minutes.

2. Stir and add the stock. Bring to the boil and simmer for 15 minutes, then add the spinach and rocket and simmer for a further 5 minutes. Season to taste with the salt and pepper.

3. Serve immediately, or cool completely then reheat gently when required. Don't boil the soup when reheating, however, as this will impair its flavour.

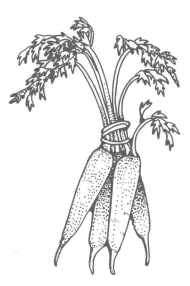

Crab Risotto

Risottos are very popular, not just because they're delicious, but also because they're very versatile. You can make them with lots of different ingredients – as shown in this example.

Serves 6 as a starter or 4 as a main course

2 tablespoons olive oil
1 onion, finely chopped
2 garlic cloves, chopped
1 litre chicken, fish or vegetable stock
400g risotto rice, such as Arborio
150ml dry white wine
400g crabmeat
Juice of 1 lemon
2 tablespoons fresh parsley, chopped
Salt and pepper to taste
½ teaspoon chilli flakes
50g butter
50g fresh Parmesan, grated
4 lemon wedges, to serve

1. Heat the oil in a pan. Fry the onion and garlic over a moderate heat.

2. Heat the stock in another pan until boiling, then turn the heat down to a gentle simmer.

3. Stir the rice into the onion and garlic mixture and stir gently to coat the rice in the flavours and oil.

4. Add the wine to the rice and simmer until it has all been absorbed.

5. Add a ladle of the stock and allow this to be absorbed before adding another. Repeat until the rice is tender – this will take about 25 minutes. The mixture should be very moist but not too runny.

6. Stir in the crabmeat, lemon juice and parsley and keep on the heat for 2 more minutes. Season with salt and pepper to taste and add the chilli flakes.

7. Remove from the heat and add the butter and Parmesan. Stir gently.

8. Serve with lemon wedges.

Spring Cabbage Dolmas

Vine leaves are the usual wrapping for this dish, but cabbage leaves work just as well. This very tasty Greek recipe can be used as a starter or main course, but it also makes excellent buffet food if you make smaller versions that can be eaten with the fingers.

Serves 4 as a main course

2 tablespoons oil
1 large onion, finely chopped
2 garlic cloves, chopped
400g minced lamb
½ teaspoon dried mint
½ teaspoon fresh rosemary leaves
1 tablespoon tomato purée mixed with 4 tablespoons water
Salt and pepper to taste
8 cabbage leaves, about 10–12cm across
150g cooked long-grain rice
1 tablespoon fresh parsley, finely chopped
1 egg, beaten
400ml chicken or vegetable stock
50ml white wine
3 tablespoons tomato purée

1. Preheat the oven to 170°C/gas mark 3.

2. Heat the oil in a saucepan over a medium heat. Fry the onions and garlic for 3 minutes, then add the meat, mint, rosemary and tomato purée mixture. Season to taste with salt and pepper.

3. Simmer for about 15 minutes. The mixture should be quite moist but not runny. Set aside.

4. Bring a large pan of salted water to the boil, then turn off the heat. Put the cabbage leaves in the water and leave for 10 minutes.

5. Meanwhile, put the rice in a bowl with the parsley and mix well. Stir in the meat mixture and add enough egg to bind the mixture together.

6. Drain the cabbage leaves and pat them dry. Lay the leaves flat in front of you with the stalk end towards you. Spoon an eighth of the meat mixture into the centre of each leaf, then fold it up: first from the stalk end, then folding the sides over to make a parcel. Place the dolmas seam-side down in a roasting tin or ovenproof dish close together so that they remain wrapped.

7. Combine the stock, wine and 3 tablespoons tomato purée in a pan, check and adjust the seasoning if necessary and bring to the boil, stirring constantly. As soon as it is boiling, carefully pour the mixture over the dolmas.

8. Cover and cook for about 50 minutes to an hour.

9. Lift the dolmas carefully out of the sauce and arrange on plates. Pour a little of the sauce over them and serve with crusty bread or potato wedges.

Sea Bass with Fresh Pesto Sauce

This recipe is a tribute to Keith Floyd, who died while this book was being written. He inspired us all to experiment and enjoy being daring about cooking, conveying his sense of humour and joy of living in his programmes and books. His original recipe used red mullet, but here, sea bass does the job beautifully.

Serves 4

For the pesto sauce
3 garlic cloves, crushed
50g pine nuts
About 20g fresh basil
3 tablespoons fresh
 chopped parsley
Salt and pepper
 to taste
6 tablespoons olive oil

For the fish
4 x 150g sea bass fillets
3 tablespoons olive oil
Juice of 1 lemon
Fresh basil and parsley
 leaves, to garnish

1. Make the pesto by pounding the garlic and pine nuts together in a mortar and pestle. Tear up the basil leaves and add to the mortar with the parsley and a little salt and pepper. Pound again and stir in the olive oil. Alternatively, put all the ingredients into a food processor and whizz together for about 20 seconds.

2. Heat the olive oil in a frying pan and fry the fish for a few minutes on each side. Place the fillets on warm plates and drizzle with lemon juice. Season if necessary and spoon the pesto evenly over the fish.

3. Garnish with some fresh basil and parsley, and serve with some pasta to mop up the pesto.

Roast Leg of Lamb in Red-wine Sauce with Rosemary Potatoes

Roast lamb is a great favourite of many in the spring, and this recipe makes it extra-special.
The rosemary potatoes go so well with this dish.

Serves 4–6

1 leg of lamb, weighing
   about 1.5–2kg
1 garlic clove,
   cut in half
Salt and pepper
   to taste
1 tablespoon
   sunflower oil
300ml warm water
300ml red wine
1 tablespoon
   redcurrant jelly
2 teaspoons cornflour
   mixed with
   3 teaspoons water
   to make a
   smooth paste

For the potatoes
4–5 medium potatoes,
   peeled and cut
   into cubes
3 sprigs rosemary;
   leaves stripped
   off the stalks
Salt and pepper
   to taste
15g butter
1 tablespoon
   sunflower oil

1. Preheat the oven to 200°C/gas mark 6

2. Place the lamb in a roasting tin and rub all over with the garlic clove. Season with salt and pepper and drizzle the oil over the meat. Pour the water around the lamb and place in the oven. Cook for 30 minutes, then remove from the oven, cover with foil and reduce the heat to 180°C/gas mark 4. Return to the oven and cook for 1–1¼ hours.

3. Lift the meat out of the oven and transfer it to a carving plate. Rest for 10 minutes before carving.

4. Pour the juices from the roasting pan into a saucepan. Pour the wine into the roasting pan and use it to deglaze the pan, then pour this liquid into the saucepan. Season to taste.

5. Stir in the redcurrant jelly and cornflour paste and bring to the boil. Stir constantly. When it thickens, turn down the heat and simmer for 1 minute. Remove from the heat.

For the potatoes
1. Boil the potatoes in salted water until tender, but still firm.

2. Drain well and put into an ovenproof dish or roasting pan.

3. Sprinkle the rosemary over the potatoes. Season to taste.

4. Melt the butter and oil together in a small pan and pour over the potatoes.

5. Put the potatoes into the oven about 25 minutes before the lamb has finished cooking. They should be cooked when you're ready to serve the meat and sauce.

Quick Salmon Pasta with Baby Leaves

This is an easy and quite economical dish. You can make it with half-fat crème fraîche if you wish.

Serves 4

1 tablespoon
   lemon juice
1x 200g salmon fillet,
   skin removed
400ml crème fraîche
1 tablespoon dill
Salt and black
   pepper to taste
500g fresh tagliatelle
Baby salad leaves
   (couple of handfuls)

1. Drizzle the lemon juice over the fish and either cook in the microwave for 2–3 minutes or bake in the oven for 5 minutes at 200°C/gas mark 6.

2. Flake the fish in a bowl and reserve any fish liquid.

3. Put the crème fraîche into a saucepan and add the dill and fish liquor. Season to taste with salt and plenty of black pepper. Stir until the sauce bubbles.

4. Add the fish and cook gently for a few minutes.

5. Meanwhile, put the tagliatelle in boiling salted water and continue to boil until cooked.

6. Drain the pasta and put it back in the pan. Pour on the sauce and stir well, but be careful not to break the pasta.

7. Serve in warm pasta bowls and top each portion with some salad leaves.

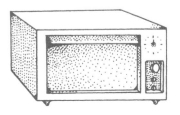

Carrageen Moss Pudding

This delightfully creamy pudding has a smooth texture. Carrageen moss is available in some health-food stores and from suppliers on the internet.

Serves 4–6

15g dried
  carrageen moss
300ml milk
1 teaspoon
  vanilla extract
25g caster sugar
2 tablespoons honey
1 egg, separated
200ml single cream
50g sultanas

1. Put the moss in sufficient warm water to cover it. Leave it to soak for 10 minutes.

2. Drain and put the moss in a saucepan with the milk and vanilla.

3. Bring to the boil, then simmer for 10 minutes.

4. Put the sugar, honey and egg yolk in a bowl and whisk until light.

5. Strain the milk and moss mixture into the sugar and egg. Push all the jelly-like substance through the sieve. Discard the leftover bits.

6. Add the cream and sultanas.

7. Whisk the egg white until stiff and fold into the creamy mixture.

8. Spoon into individual ramekin dishes and chill for 1½ hours before serving.

Honey Cake

A versatile cake that can be eaten on its own or spread with your favourite preserve.

Makes 6–8 portions

180g butter
100g golden
    caster sugar
2 tablespoons
    clear honey
220g self-raising
    flour, sieved
4 small eggs, beaten
Zest and juice of a
    blood orange

1. Grease and line an 18cm diameter cake tin and preheat the oven to 170°C/gas mark 3.

2. Cream the butter, sugar and honey together until pale and fluffy.

3. Add 2 tablespoons of the flour and then gradually beat in the eggs.

4. Fold in the flour along with the zest and juice of the blood orange.

5. Spoon the mixture into the tin.

6. Bake for 45 minutes. Reduce the oven temperature to 150°C/gas mark 2 and bake for 45 minutes more. Test the cake to see if it is cooked by pushing a metal skewer through the middle. If cooked, the skewer will come out clean. If not, bake for 5 more minutes and test again.

7. Cool for 10 minutes in the tin before removing. Leave the paper on for 10 more minutes before removing it. Store in an airtight tin.

Elderflower Jelly

This delicately flavoured preserve uses apples as the main 'carrier' for the flavour of the elderflowers.

Makes 3–4 x 450g jars

2kg cooking apples
20 elderflower heads
Juice of 3 lemons
75g sugar to every
    100ml of juice

1. Roughly chop the apples – don't peel or core them.

2. Put them in a pan with the flowers and sufficient water to cover.

3. Bring to the boil, then simmer for 30 minutes. Mash the fruit to break it up.

4. Pour the mixture into a jelly bag standing over a large bowl and allow it to drain through overnight. Do not squeeze the fruit through as this will spoil the appearance of the jelly.

5. Next morning, discard the solids. Measure the juice.

6. Weigh out the required amount of sugar. If the volume of juice is 680ml, for example, then use 450g sugar for the 600ml plus about 50g for the 80ml. If the volume measures 820ml, use 600g sugar plus about 10g for the 20ml.

7. Place the strained juice, lemon juice and sugar in a large preserving pan and heat gently, stirring constantly until the sugar has dissolved.

8. Bring to the boil and boil for 10–15 minutes, then test the jelly for setting point (see page 19). Pour into sterilised jars, then label and date.

Rosemary and Mint Jelly

This makes an excellent accompaniment to lamb dishes and can be made very quickly.

Makes 2 x 450g jars

300ml apple juice
150ml malt vinegar
450g jam sugar
3 tablespoons fresh
   mint, chopped
3 sprigs rosemary,
   leaves only,
   roughly chopped

1. Put the apple juice and vinegar in a pan and bring to the boil.

2. Remove from the heat and stir in the sugar.

3. Return to the heat and bring to the boil, stirring constantly. Boil for 4 minutes, then add the mint and rosemary. Stir and remove from the heat.

4. Allow to cool for 10 minutes, then stir to distribute the herbs. Pot into sterilised jars, label and date.

Dandelion Tea

Dandelion is a proven natural diuretic. It is also said to be good for digestion and bloating, so this is a cleansing drink.

Makes 2 cups

10 heads of
   dandelion flowers
4–5 young dandelion
   leaves, chopped
About 500ml
   boiling water
1 teaspoon honey

1. Wash all the plant parts well, then put them in a teapot.

2. Boil the water and pour it over the flowers and leaves. Stir well, stir in the honey and cover the teapot with a cosy. Leave for 15 minutes to allow the flavour to develop.

3. Strain the tea as you pour it into cups and drink immediately.

As a child, May was the time of Whitsun walks – an excuse to dress up and join the throngs of walkers. Now it is a sign that summer's on its way, a herald of the abundance of produce it will bring. There are the delights of smelling the fresh morning air tinged with sunshine, or the evening showers, welcome after a hot afternoon.

The first quiet rush of summer is characterised by a massive increase in the insect population – and, of course, slugs and snails. You could say that gastropod gastronomy was 'in season' from now on, and why not? They eat our precious lettuces and radishes so quickly, so why shouldn't we eat them?

Yet there are millions of reasons why we should leave them; hens devour them, for one, and promptly convert them into eggs. As the days lengthen, the little combs on point-of-lay chickens fill with fresh blood and become bright red, as if someone had turned a light bulb on in their heads. The tiny red-light district of many a backyard is soothed by gentle *bok-boking*.

The season of eggs lasts from May to November, and each hen should give a glorious egg each day. Glorious, indeed: until you've tasted a fresh egg, collected and cooked for breakfast within a few minutes, you will never really appreciate what it means to have fresh – really fresh – food.

May

May Menu

A three-course meal to serve 4–6 people

Asparagus Soup

Dover Sole with Samphire Tempura

Strawberry Mousse Cheesecake

Asparagus Soup

A firm favourite for asparagus–lovers, especially as the season is so short. Make the most of it!

50g butter
1 onion, finely chopped
250g asparagus,
   chopped into
   1cm pieces
1 level tablespoon
   plain flour
1 litre vegetable or
   chicken stock
Salt and pepper
   to taste
About 500ml milk
100ml single cream

1. Melt the butter in a large pan over a low heat and add the onions. Fry gently for 2–3 minutes until translucent.

2. Add all the asparagus except for 4–6 heads. Allow to sweat in the butter with the onions for a few minutes.

3. Sprinkle in the flour and stir well.

4. Add the stock gradually, stirring it in thoroughly. Bring to the boil and stir.

5. Turn down the heat and simmer for 10 minutes. Season to taste with salt and pepper.

6. Blend or liquidise the soup and return to the pan. Add the milk to give the desired thickness and heat to just boiling, stirring constantly.

7. Swirl in the cream and ladle into soup bowls. Float an asparagus head on top of each bowl of soup and serve.

Dover Sole with Samphire Tempura

Sole is a delicately flavoured fish and goes well with samphire – which is why this dish is a real taste of the sea. The secret of light, crispy tempura batter is to not over-whisk and to use it immediately.

Olive oil
12 small Dover
   sole fillets
Salt and pepper
   to taste
Juice of 1 lemon
80g plain flour
1 rounded teaspoon
   cornflour
180ml ice-cold water
200g samphire, washed
   and trimmed into
   equal lengths

1. Heat the grill and sprinkle a little olive oil onto a baking sheet. Season the fish with salt and pepper to taste and squeeze over the lemon juice. Place the fillets on the sheet.

2. Drizzle a little olive oil over the fish and place the fillets under the grill for about 5 minutes.

3. Make the tempura batter by sieving the 2 flours, salt and pepper together in a bowl and whisk in the ice-cold water gradually. Don't worry if it is a bit a lumpy; just don't overbeat it.

4. Heat more olive oil in a deep pan until very hot, dip the samphire into the batter and lower each piece carefully into the hot oil. Fry in small batches, lifting out when just golden and crisp.

5. Drain on kitchen paper and serve immediately with the sole.

Strawberry Mousse Cheesecake

This simple yet deliciously impressive dessert can be made early and chilled until ready to serve.

300g digestive biscuits
120g butter
300g strawberries
2 teaspoons
  icing sugar
100ml double cream
100g mascarpone
  cheese
3 egg whites
50g caster sugar

1. Butter a 22cm loose-bottomed (springform) tin.

2. Crush the digestive biscuits. The easiest way to do this is by putting them in a polythene bag and using a rolling pin. Place the crumbs in a bowl.

3. Melt the butter in a pan and pour it over the biscuit crumbs; stir well to combine. Press the biscuit mixture into the base of the tin and firm down well. Chill for 1 hour.

4. Put the strawberries and the icing sugar in a blender and whizz to a purée.

5. In a bowl, combine the cream and mascarpone and whisk for about 30 seconds. The mixture should be thick but not stiff.

6. Whisk the egg whites until they form stiff peaks, then fold in the sugar.

7. Fold the strawberry purée into the cream mixture, then do the same with the egg whites.

8. Spread the mixture over the biscuit base and smooth out the top.

9. Chill for 2–3 hours at least – the longer the better. The top won't set as firmly as a baked cheesecake so take care when serving. Serve with some extra fresh whole or halved strawberries.

Watercress Soup

This peppery plant makes a wonderful soup when combined with potato and hint of nutmeg.

Serves 4

25g butter
1 onion, chopped
2 garlic cloves,
   chopped
2 medium potatoes,
   peeled and cubed
700ml chicken stock
2 large bunches
   watercress, about
   250g, washed, and
   roughly chopped
   (but reserve a few
   leaves to garnish)
A little grated nutmeg
Salt and pepper
   to taste

1. Melt the butter in a saucepan and fry the onion gently until it is soft. Stir in the garlic.

2. Add the potato and continue to fry gently for 4 minutes.

3. Pour in the stock and bring to the boil, then simmer for 10 minutes, or until the potatoes are tender.

4. Add the watercress, keeping a few leaves to garnish the soup, and simmer for 5 minutes. Add the nutmeg and any other seasoning.

5. Liquidise until it is as smooth as you wish.

6. Serve in bowls garnished with a few watercress leaves and some crusty bread.

Asparagus with Soft Cheese Sauce

Another asparagus recipe, which is delicious as a light lunch.

Serves as many as you like!

4 asparagus spears
 per person
A knob of butter
100g light soft
 cream cheese
2 tablespoons
 single cream
2 tablespoons milk
Salt and white pepper
 to taste
1 thinly sliced piece
 of wholemeal bread
 per person, toasted,
 buttered and cut
 into quarters

1. Steam the asparagus for 3–5 minutes, depending on size. Drain and coat in a knob of butter.

2. Make the sauce: put the cream cheese, cream and milk into a small saucepan. Heat gently, stirring constantly until they all combine. Season to taste.

3. Place the cooked asparagus on a small plate and cover it with the sauce.

4. Serve with the wholemeal toast.

Artichokes in Hot Garlic Dressing

This make a wonderful starter course. Be sure to use very young artichokes.

Serves 6

6 small globe
   artichokes
Juice of 3 lemons; you
   may need a little
   more during cooking
   time so have another
   lemon ready
6 tablespoons olive oil
2 garlic cloves, grated
1 teaspoon chopped
   fresh marjoram
Salt and black pepper
   to taste

1. Cut the artichokes into quarters. Remove the chokes and place in very cold water and lemon juice so that they don't brown.

2. Make the dressing by whisking together the lemon juice, olive oil, garlic, marjoram and salt and pepper.

3. Drain the artichokes and put them into a heavy-based lidded saucepan. Pour over the dressing and heat until simmering. Cover and cook gently over a low heat for 15–20 minutes. Shake the pan to mix the contents and stop them catching on the bottom.

4. Remove the lid after 15 minutes and check to see if the artichokes are cooking evenly. Add a little more lemon juice if necessary.

5. Arrange the artichokes on warm plates and spoon the hot dressing over the top. Serve with chunks of fresh crusty bread.

Smoked Haddock Kedgeree with Runner Beans

Serves 4

400g long-grain rice
100g young runner
    beans, sliced, any
    stringy bits removed
300g smoked haddock
Milk, for poaching
20g butter
1 tablespoon
    sunflower oil
1 dessertspoon
    turmeric
1 teaspoon
    ground cumin
½ teaspoon ground
    coriander
1 teaspoon medium
    curry powder
3 hard-boiled
    eggs, shelled
1 tablespoon
    chopped parsley

1. Boil the rice as usual until almost cooked, then add the runner beans for the last 3 minutes of cooking time.

2. Meanwhile, poach the haddock in a little milk – enough to 'hold' the fish but not cover it. Cook for about 4 minutes. Lift out the fish, set aside on a plate and flake. Boil the poaching liquid vigorously until it has reduced by half.

3. Drain the rice and beans and leave them in a colander.

4. Heat the butter and oil in a frying pan and add the spices. Heat for a few seconds.

5. Add the rice and beans and stir well to coat in the spicy butter.

6. Add the fish and the reduced poaching stock and cook for about 4 minutes, stirring gently to coat everything in the sauce.

7. Chop the eggs and stir into the kedgeree. Sprinkle with the chopped parsley and serve immediately.

Pork and Baby Broad Bean Stir-fry

A quick and healthy dish that uses the youngest broad beans.

Serves 4

1 tablespoon
sesame oil
1 tablespoon
sunflower oil
Half an onion,
thinly chopped
4 spring onions, sliced
into thin strips
450g lean pork steak,
cut into thin strips
2 garlic cloves,
chopped
2–3 baby radishes,
sliced thinly, and a
couple of the leaves,
roughly chopped
2 tablespoons soy
sauce mixed with
3 tablespoons water
2 tablespoons rice
wine or dry sherry
100g baby broad beans

1. Heat the oils in a wok or large frying pan until hot.

2. Add the onion and spring onions and fry for 1 minute.

3. Add the pork and garlic and stir-fry until the pork is cooked.

4. Add the radishes and leaves and stir well.

5. Add the soy sauce mixture, rice wine and the broad beans and stir everything together while frying.

6. Serve immediately with Chinese egg noodles, which, if cooked, may be added to the pork and beans and stirred together before serving.

Lamb and Spinach Curry

A mildly spiced curry dish that is delicious served with boiled basmati rice.

Serves 4

25g butter
1 medium onion, sliced
2 sticks celery,
    chopped
800g diced lamb
1 x 400g can tomatoes
2 tablespoon
    tomato purée
2 garlic cloves,
    chopped
2 dessertspoons mild
    curry powder
1 level teaspoon
    turmeric
1 level teaspoon
    ground cumin
1 tablespoon chopped
    fresh mint
750ml vegetable or
    beef stock
4 tablespoons
    red lentils
Salt and black pepper
    to taste
100g spinach leaves
4 tablespoons
    natural yogurt

1. Melt the butter in a pan and fry the onion and celery gently for 2 minutes.

2. Add the lamb and brown all over.

3. Add the tomatoes, the tomato purée, garlic, curry powder, turmeric, cumin and mint and stir into the meat; cook gently to allow the flavours to develop.

4. Pour over the stock, cover and simmer for 50 minutes.

5. Stir well and add the lentils and any necessary salt and pepper. Simmer for a further 20 minutes.

6. Stir in the spinach and cook for 5 minutes, or until the leaves have wilted into the curry.

7. Serve with rice and some plain natural yogurt swirled onto the top.

Crusted Salmon in Dill Sauce with Jersey Royals

The three main elements of this dish – salmon, dill and little Jersey Royal potatoes – make an ideal combination.

Serves 4

150ml milk
4 x 150g salmon fillets
100g breadcrumbs
½ teaspoon salt
2 teaspoons chopped
    fresh dill
2–3 tablespoons
    olive oil
Black pepper to taste
750g Jersey Royal
    potatoes, boiled
    until tender
A knob of butter

For the sauce

The poaching milk
    from the salmon
250ml single cream
50ml white wine
3 tablespoons
    chopped dill
Juice of 1 lemon
Pinch of salt

1. Pour the milk in a large pan and put in the salmon fillets. Bring to the boil, then simmer for 4 minutes.

2. Remove the fish from the liquid and put onto an oiled baking sheet. Preheat the oven to 190°C/gas mark 5.

3. Make the crust: put the breadcrumbs in a bowl and stir in the salt and chopped dill. Pour in the oil and combine well; add enough oil so that the breadcrumbs cling together but the mixture isn't too oily.

4. Spoon the crust mixture onto the salmon and press it down well. Place the fish in the oven and cook in the hottest part until the crust is golden – about 12 minutes.

5. Make the sauce while the salmon cooks. Combine the poaching milk, cream, wine, dill, lemon juice and salt in a pan and bring slowly to the boil, then turn down the heat and simmer for 5 minutes.

6. Serve the hot sauce with the salmon. If you prefer a crispy crust, pour the sauce in a jug and let everyone help themselves. Serve with the Jersey potatoes, coated in the butter.

Poached Egg with Jersey Royals and Smoky Bacon

This tasty dish can be served for lunch or brunch, and you could replace the bacon with chopped chorizo for a change.

Serves 4

1 tablespoon
 sunflower oil
6 rashers smoky
 bacon, chopped
750g baby Jersey Royal
 potatoes, washed
 and boiled until
 just tender
2 tablespoons
 chopped chives
4 eggs
Salt and pepper
 to taste

1. Heat the oil in a frying pan and fry the bacon until it begins to crisp.

2. Add the potatoes and chives and fry them with the bacon for 3–4 minutes. Place in a dish to keep warm in the oven.

3. Poach the eggs whichever way you find easiest.

4. Spoon some of the potato and bacon mixture onto a plate, sprinkle each with some chives and top with the egg. Season with salt and pepper to taste and serve immediately.

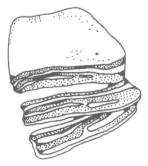

Strawberry Ice Cream

Who can resist the taste of fresh strawberries and ice cream? The best news is that this ice cream is a combination of both.

Makes about 1.2 litres

4 whole eggs
2 egg yolks
150g caster sugar
300ml double cream
300ml whole milk
500g strawberries,
   washed and hulled
2 tablespoons
   icing sugar

1. Whisk together the eggs, yolks and sugar.

2. Heat the cream and milk in a saucepan, whisking gently. When the cream is hot (not boiling), remove it from the heat and stir in the egg mixture.

3. Return to the heat and cook the custard, whisking gently and continuously, until the mixture thickens. This will take about 10–12 minutes.

4. Remove from the heat and leave to stand while you prepare the strawberries. To stop a skin from forming on the custard, place a disc of greaseproof paper on the top while it cools.

5. Halve the strawberries and put them in a saucepan together with the icing sugar. Heat gently until the juice of the fruit begins to run freely. Use a potato masher to mash the strawberries while still on the heat.

6. Cook for 3 minutes, then pour into a bowl and allow to cool.

7. Stir the strawberries into the custard mixture, which should also be cool and thick by now. Beat together if you like a smoother ice cream, or just stir it in so you have bits of strawberry in the ice cream.

8. Put the ice cream into a freezer-proof container for 1 hour, then remove it, stir to break up any large ice crystals, and return it to the freezer. After another hour, repeat the stirring, then leave to freeze. This is a firm ice cream and will need about 10 minutes in the fridge to soften before serving.

Strawberry Shortcake

A scrumptious dessert that is suitable for any occasion.

Serves 8

For the shortcake
130g butter
100g golden
   caster sugar
80g plain flour
80g self-raising flour
20g ground almonds

For the top
250g strawberries,
   hulled
1 tablespoon golden
   caster sugar
100ml whipping cream

1. Grease a 20cm sandwich tin. Preheat the oven to 180°C/gas mark 4.

2. Cream the butter and sugar together until fluffy.

3. Sift the two flours together into the cream mixture and fold in. Stir in the ground almonds.

4. Spoon the mixture into the prepared tin and bake for 15–20 minutes, or until light golden in colour.

5. Transfer to a cooling rack and leave in the tin until cool.

For the top
1. Slice the strawberries and put in a bowl. Sprinkle with the sugar.

2. Whip the cream until it form soft peaks. Put the shortcake onto a serving plate and spread it with the cream.

3. Arrange the strawberries on top of the cream. Serve immediately or chill until needed.

Scones with Strawberry Jam and Cream

An English classic. The recipe makes plain scones; add 30g of raisins or sultanas to the mixture just after rubbing in the butter if you prefer them with fruit. If you're eating them straight away, allow ten minutes' cooling time as they are impossible to slice in half if they're too hot!

Makes about 12 scones

450g self-raising flour
1 level teaspoon salt
1 tablespoon golden caster sugar
60g butter, chopped into small pieces
1 tablespoon lemon juice
400ml milk

1. Preheat oven to 220°C/gas mark 7.

2. Sift the flour and salt together in a mixing bowl. Stir in the sugar.

3. Add the butter and rub it lightly into the flour with your fingertips until the mixture looks like fine breadcrumbs.

4. Add the lemon juice to the milk and stir vigorously. The milk should begin to thicken slightly. Mix this into the flour with a fork using light, quick strokes. This should form a soft, pliable dough.

5. Bring the dough together by kneading lightly.

6. Press the dough out on a floured surface to about 2.5cm thick. Using either a fluted or plain cookie cutter, press straight down into the dough without twisting the cutter (if you twist, your scone won't rise as much). Each time you make another shape, dip your cutter into a little flour; this will make removing the cutter easier.

7. Place each scone on a lightly oiled baking tray and brush the tops with a little milk.

8. Bake for 20 minutes, or until they are golden brown.

9. Cool and serve with strawberry jam (see page 98), or any of your favourite preserves, and a spoonful of clotted cream.

Strawberry Jam

This is an easy jam to make to serve with your scones. It will keep unopened for up to one year.

Makes 4 x 450g jars

1kg strawberries,
   washed and hulled
Juice of 1 lemon
1 x 13g sachet pectin
1kg white
   granulated sugar

1. Put the strawberries in a large pan over a medium heat. Use a masher to squash down some of the fruit, but leave some whole to add texture to the finished jam. Add the lemon juice.

2. Bring the fruit to a fast simmer and cook for 2–3 minutes, or until some of strawberries are soft. Lower the heat slightly.

3. Sprinkle in the pectin and the sugar and stir until all the sugar is dissolved. Bring to the boil and cook at boiling for 4 minutes.

4. Remove from the heat and test for setting point (see page 19). If it isn't ready, boil for 30 seconds longer and repeat the test.

5. As soon as the setting point is reached, remove the jam from the heat, stir and leave to cool for 5 minutes.

6. Stir to distribute the fruit before ladling into sterilised jars. Seal the jars immediately and label when cool.

Strawberry Sauce

This easy-to-make sauce is wonderful with many desserts and puddings, but it goes particularly well with ice cream.

350g strawberries,
  hulled and chopped
2 rounded tablespoons
  caster sugar
4 tablespoons water

1. Put all the ingredients in a pan and bring slowly to the boil.

2. Turn down the heat and simmer gently until the strawberries are soft.

3. Push the mixture through a sieve and test for sweetness; if you like it sweeter add a teaspoon of icing sugar and stir.

4. Pour the sauce into a jug and serve.

Elderflower Champagne No. 1

Here are two very different recipes for elderflower champagne. The first makes a full-bodied, strong, wine-type drink. The second is lightly alcoholic and much more refreshing. Both are worth making to use the abundance of elderflowers available, because they taste so good!

Makes about 5 litres

4 large elderflower florets
5 litres of boiling water
1kg granulated white sugar
200ml white-wine concentrate
5g citric acid
1 cup of strong tea
Wine yeast

1. Strip the flowers off the stalks with a fork into a sterile bucket.

2. Add the boiling water and stir four or five times over the next day.

3. Dissolve the sugar into 500ml boiling water to make a sugar syrup.

4. Strain the cool liquid through muslin into a second bucket and add the sugar syrup.

5. Transfer the liquid to a demijohn and add all the other ingredients, giving the vessel a good shake to mix. If the demijohn needs to be topped up, use cool boiled water.

6. Close the vessel with an airlock and stand it on a tray in case the wine spills out when fermentation starts.

7. When the bubbling has fully stopped, siphon off the liquid into a clean sterilised demijohn, being careful to leave the gunge behind in the bottom. Top up with apple juice or boiled water. Close the new vessel off with an airlock.

8. Leave for about six months (if you can bear to), then rack off the wine into sterilised bottles.

Elderflower Champagne No. 2

You don't need demijohns for this one. Buy two 2-litre plastic bottles of lemonade, and just before the liquid is ready to bottle, pour out the lemonade.

Makes about 4 litres

6 elderflower heads
4 litres boiling water
750g sugar
Juice of 2 lemons

1. Put the elderflower heads and lemons into a sterile bucket and pour on the boiling water. Cover the bucket with a tea towel and leave to soak for 24 hours.

2. Strain the liquid through muslin and add the sugar and lemon juice. Stir until the sugar is completely dissolved, then pour into two 2-litre screwtop lemonade bottles.

3. Leave the tops slightly loose for a couple of weeks.

4. Allow to mature for 3 months before drinking. Serve cool when ready to drink.

June signals the beginning of a season of abundance. Fruit and vegetables are literally bursting out. Strawberries and Wimbledon go hand in hand, as do asparagus and almost every other food there is. Every Englishman should eat asparagus in June. True, the season does start in May, but the best flavour is found in those spears that push through the earth in June. Somehow they seem more succulent – especially if it has been raining.

Another fruit to die for in June is the marvellously aromatic cherry, although it isn't really comforting to know that the flavour of cherries and almonds comes from the cyanide in the makeup of the fruit. However, this just goes to show that a little of what you fancy, etc – but the fact remains that there is enough cyanide in a pound of cherries to kill a mouse. Perhaps that's why you never see a mouse actually eating a pound of cherries, glacé or otherwise!

Nature has turned the heat on in June, everything is growing fast and farmers and gardeners all wait for rain. The first new potatoes of the year, planted some 18 weeks earlier before St Patrick's Day, are swollen by a good soaking. You cannot underestimate the joy of plunging your fork into the ground, not knowing how wonderful your 'First Earlies' will be.

'Pentland Javelin' need around 18 weeks to produce a good enough crop. Around the middle of June they can be unearthed and, cooked within minutes of seeing the sunlight, they need no other attention than a little salt and pepper and maybe a blob of butter – just the right partner for a plate of fresh white fish.

June

June Menu
A three-course meal to serve 4 people

∽

Fish Fritto Misto

∽

Honey-glazed Tenderloin

∽

Strawberry and Champagne Jellies with Chantilly Cream

Fish Fritto Misto

Fritto misto is Italian for 'fried mixture', and you can make it with any type of seafood. This version uses simple strips of fish and whole sardines.

1 x 80–100g fillet each
of salmon, haddock,
cod, plaice, halibut
and trout
Oil for frying
100g plain white flour
½ teaspoon salt
½ teaspoon
cayenne pepper
8 sardines
100ml milk

1. Cut the fish fillets into strips; trout and plaice may need to be cut into wider pieces as they are thin.

2. Heat sufficient oil in a deep pan to deep-fry.

3. Sieve the flour, salt and cayenne pepper into a bowl and put the milk into a bowl next to the flour.

4. First cook the sardines by dipping them into the milk, then into the seasoned flour, then putting them straight into the hot oil. Cook until golden and crisp – about 4 minutes. Fry the fish in batches of four. Put on a plate with a layer of kitchen paper and keep warm.

5. Dip the strips of fish in the same way as the sardines and fry, again in small batches. Fry the strips for 2–3 minutes, or until golden.

6. Serve as soon as the last batch is cooked with lemon wedges and freshly made lemon mayonnaise (see page 66).

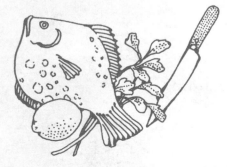

Honey-glazed Pork Tenderloin

Tenderloin is a very lean cut of meat, so it needs care when roasting. This recipe wraps the meat and flavours together in rashers of streaky bacon, which keep it moist and tender.

400–450g pork fillet
  or tenderloin
1 tablespoon soy sauce
4–5 rashers unsmoked
  streaky bacon

For the marinade
2 tablespoons honey
1 tablespoon
  sunflower oil
2 teaspoons
  Dijon mustard
1 tablespoon soft
  brown sugar
½ teaspoon freshly
  ground black pepper

1. Make the marinade by putting all the ingredients together in a bowl and whisking with a balloon whisk.

2. Brush the marinade all over the pork and massage it into the meat with your hands. Make a few holes in the pork with a skewer to allow the marinade to get deeper into the meat. Put the meat into a roasting pan and cover with the rest of the marinade. Cover with foil and leave to marinate for 2 hours.

3. Preheat the oven to 200°C/gas mark 6.

4. After the 2 hours, drizzle the pork with the soy sauce and leave for 10 minutes.

5. Lift the meat out of the marinade and wrap the bacon rashers firmly around it, overlapping them so there are no gaps.

6. Put back in the roasting pan, cover with foil and place in the oven. Cook for 20 minutes, then remove the foil and cook for 10–15 minutes.

7. Transfer the meat to a plate and allow to rest for 15 minutes before carving.

Serving suggestion
Serve with boiled new potatoes and broccoli.

Strawberry and Champagne Jellies with Chantilly Cream

This summery, light and refreshing dessert is definitely an adult jelly.

200g caster sugar
250ml water
450g strawberries
12g powdered gelatine
300ml Champagne

For the Chantilly cream
200ml double cream
1 level tablespoon
  icing sugar
½ teaspoon
  vanilla extract

1. Put the sugar and water in a saucepan and bring to the boil, stirring until all the sugar has dissolved. Remove from the heat.

2. Reserve 4 as a garnish and purée the strawberries with a potato masher or a hand blender. They need to be as smooth as possible.

3. Put the purée in a bowl with the sugar syrup and allow to cool completely.

4. Pass the strawberry mixture through a sieve to get rid of seeds and really hard bits.

5. Put the gelatine in a little bowl and cover with 4 tablespoons of water. Stir and leave for 5 minutes.

6. Pour the Champagne over the strawberry mixture and stir well.

7. Put about 50ml of the strawberry mixture into a pan with the gelatine and heat gently to make sure the gelatine has dissolved. Do not boil.

8. Pour the gelatine mixture into the fruit and stir well.

9. Pour the jelly into a large jelly mould and place it in the fridge to set for at least 2 hours. Garnish the top with the fresh strawberries before serving with Chantilly cream.

For the Chantilly cream
1. Put the cream into a bowl and sift in the icing sugar.

2. Add the vanilla and whisk everything together until it forms soft peaks.

3. Chill for 30 minutes before serving with the jelly.

Broccoli and Cauliflower Soup

The crispy bacon pieces on top really give this soup an added zing. It's a great way to use any cauliflowers that have become too open-headed.

Serves 4–6

50g butter
1 small cauliflower,
  divided into florets
300g broccoli, divided
  into florets
1 large or 2 small
  carrots, chopped
2 celery sticks,
  chopped
Half a small onion,
  finely chopped
4 tablespoons chopped
  fresh parsley
2 sprigs thyme
1 litre vegetable or
  chicken stock
Salt and pepper
  to taste
100ml milk
100ml cream
Cooked crispy bacon
  pieces, to serve

1. Melt the butter gently in a large pan and add all the vegetables. Cover and sweat them for 15 minutes on a very low heat.

2. Add the herbs and stock and bring to the boil. Turn down the heat and simmer for 15 minutes. Season with salt and pepper.

3. Add the milk and simmer for 10 minutes.

4. Blend the soup until it is as smooth as you like it, then stir in the cream.

5. Reheat if necessary, and serve with the bacon pieces on top.

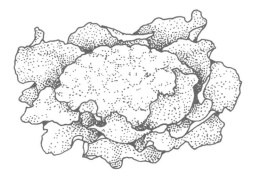

Brie and Radish Mousse

Many people aren't fond of radishes in a salad, but they should still love this creamy mousse. The radishes give it a wonderfully peppery taste.

Serves 4

250g ripe Brie
300ml double cream
16 radishes, chopped,
   except for 2 which
   should be very thinly
   sliced for garnishing

1. Remove as much of the rind from the Brie as you can. Put the cheese into a bowl with 50ml of the cream, then beat them together.

2. Fold the chopped radishes into the cheese mixture.

3. Whisk the rest of the cream until it forms stiff peaks, then fold into the cheese mixture.

4. Spoon the mixture into 4 ramekins and top with a few slices of radish.

5. Chill for 2 hours before serving with crackers or other biscuits for cheese.

Sea Trout Pâté with Melba Toast

This is a quick and easy recipe. You can make it with full- or half-fat soft cheese – the choice is up to you.

Serves 2–4

For the pâté
2 x 200g sea
   trout fillets
200g soft cream
   cheese
2 tablespoons
   lemon juice
1 tablespoon fresh
   chopped parsley

For the toast
2 slices of white or
   brown bread
Butter for spreading
   (optional)

1. Put all the pâté ingredients into a food processor and blend together until smooth.

2. Toast the bread, then use your bread knife to slice each piece in half through the crust edge so that you have 4 very thin slices of half-toasted bread. Toast the raw side until just crisp and serve immediately with the pâté.

New Potato Salad

New potato salad can be an accompaniment to cold sliced meats or pies, or serve it as a buffet party dish.

Serves 4–6

6 rashers of bacon,
   chopped
500g small new
   potatoes
2 tablespoons chives
2 tablespoons olive oil
½ teaspoon soft
   brown sugar
2 tablespoons
   white-wine vinegar
Salt and pepper
   to taste

1. Fry the bacon in a sturdy frying pan with little (or preferably no) oil. Allow to crisp, then set aside on a plate.

2. Wash and halve but don't peel the potatoes. Boil in sufficient salted water just to cover. When tender, drain and allow to cool.

3. Put the potatoes, bacon and chives in a bowl and mix together.

4. Whisk the oil, sugar and vinegar together and pour over the potato mixture. Season to taste, and serve.

Asparagus Salad

New potatoes in their skins and served with butter make an excellent accompaniment to this dish.

Serves 4

400g asparagus
50g soft brown
    sugar dissolved in
    1 tablespoon
    boiling water
60ml white-wine
    vinegar
1 tablespoon
    chopped chervil
2 teaspoons
    chopped chives
Salt and pepper
    to taste

1. Boil the asparagus until just tender. Drain and leave to cool.

2. In a small pan, heat the sugar and vinegar until just hot. Add the herbs and season to taste. Cool.

3. Put the asparagus in a serving dish and pour the dressing on top.

4. Serve with Lemon Chicken (see page 113).

Courgette and Aubergine Bake

A tasty supper dish that can be made beforehand and reheated.

Serves 4

25g butter
1 small onion
1 garlic clove, grated
4 tablespoons tomato
   purée mixed with 6
   tablespoons of water
6 courgettes, trimmed
   and sliced thinly
   lengthways
1 small aubergine,
   trimmed and
   sliced thinly
100g Cheddar, grated
100g breadcrumbs

1. Butter an ovenproof dish. Preheat the oven to 190°C/gas mark 5.

2. Melt the butter in a small frying pan and add the onions. Fry gently until soft and stir in the garlic and tomato purée mixture. Stir and remove from the heat.

3. Put a layer of courgette then a layer of aubergine in the prepared dish and pour half of the tomato and onion mixture over the top. Repeat this, finishing with the tomato mixture.

4. Combine the grated cheese and breadcrumbs and sprinkle over the top.

5. Bake in the oven for 25 minutes. If the top isn't brown enough, finish under a hot grill. Serve with crusty bread.

Lemon Chicken

Lemon and chicken marry well in this quick and easy dish.

Serves 4

Juice of 2 lemons
2 garlic cloves, finely
   chopped or grated
4 tablespoons
   sunflower or
   olive oil
4 chicken breasts

1. In a jug or bowl, combine the lemon juice, garlic and oil.

2. Pour the marinade over the chicken and leave to infuse for at least 30 minutes.

3. Put the chicken on a baking sheet that will fit under the grill. Spoon the marinade over the chicken and grill for 5 minutes on both sides. Keep spooning the lemon mixture over the chicken as it cooks.

4. Serve with Asparagus Salad (see page 111).

Salmon and Asparagus Parcel

This makes an excellent picnic dish.

Serves 2

2 x 180g salmon fillets
8 asparagus spears
250g puff pastry
1 tablespoon
   lemon juice
Salt and black pepper
   to taste
1 tablespoon
   chopped dill
1 egg mixed with
   1 tablespoon milk,
   to glaze

1. Put the fillets on an oiled baking sheet and bake for 10 minutes at 190°C/gas mark 5.

2. Boil the asparagus for 3 minutes. Drain.

3. Roll out the pastry into a rectangle measuring about 20cm x 35cm.

4. Flake the cooked fish into a bowl, discarding any skin, and drizzle it with the lemon juice. Season with salt and pepper to taste.

5. Spoon the fish down the centre of the pastry and sprinkle the dill evenly over it.

6. Lay the asparagus on top of the salmon and dill. Preheat the oven to 200°C/gas mark 6.

7. Moisten the edges of the pastry, bring them up and over the filling and press together. Turn the edges over to secure and do the same with the ends of the parcel.

8. Lay the parcel on a greased baking sheet and brush generously with the egg and milk mixture. Make 3 slashes in the top of the pastry to allow steam to escape.

9. Bake for 30–40 minutes, or until the pastry is well-risen and golden brown in colour. Serve with salad leaves dressed with lemon juice.

Herb and Courgette Focaccia

The perfect bread for a picnic or to accompany soups.

500g strong
white flour
½ teaspoon salt
1 teaspoon each
chopped parsley,
thyme and rosemary
1 x 7g sachet
fast-action
dried yeast
2 tablespoons olive oil,
plus more for
drizzling over the
finished bread
180ml warm water
1 thinly sliced
courgette
20g coarse sea salt

1. Put the flour into a bowl and stir in the salt and herbs. Stir in the yeast.

2. Add the oil and the water and mix thoroughly.

3. Knead the dough for about 10 minutes, or until it is smooth and elastic. Leave to prove in a warm place for 40 minutes.

4. Preheat the oven to 225°C/gas mark 7.

5. After proving, press out the dough onto an oiled baking tray until it is about 2cm thick.

6. Press your fingertips into the dough to make indentations and drizzle on the extra olive oil.

7. Put the courgette slices on top of the dough. Sprinkle with sea salt and bake for about 25 minutes until golden brown.

8. Drizzle more oil over the hot bread. Allow to cool and cut into rectangles to serve.

Moussaka

A dish to serve when the weather is a bit dull or rainy. It lifts the spirits and makes real comfort food, but without being too heavy. This dish is easier to handle if you leave it to settle for five minutes before serving.

Serves 4

For the meat sauce
400g aubergines, thinly
  sliced lengthways
Salt and pepper
  to taste
Olive oil for frying
1 large onion, chopped
400–450g minced lamb
2 garlic cloves, chopped
1 tablespoon plain flour
1 x 220g can
  chopped tomatoes
125ml dry white wine
½ teaspoon each dried
  oregano and basil
3 tablespoons
  tomato purée
400g courgettes,
  sliced lengthways
100g fresh breadcrumbs

For the white sauce
15g butter
1 tablespoon flour
300ml milk
100g grated Cheddar,
  plus extra for topping
1 egg yolk
Salt and black pepper
  to taste

1. Sprinkle the strips of aubergines with salt and leave in a colander to allow some of the liquid to drain away – about 30 minutes.

2. Heat the oil in a frying pan and fry the onions until soft. Add the lamb and garlic and cook until the lamb is lightly brown.

3. Sprinkle on the flour and stir in the tomatoes, wine, herbs and tomato purée. Season to taste and simmer gently for 25–30 minutes.

4. Rinse and pat the aubergines dry with kitchen paper or a clean tea cloth. Fry them quickly, a few at a time, until they are slightly brown on one side. Do the same with the courgettes.

5. Layer a buttered dish with the meat mixture, then the aubergines and courgette and repeat, finishing with a layer of meat.

6. Make the white sauce by melting the butter in a pan over a gentle heat; stir in the flour. Remove from the heat and gradually whisk or beat in the milk.

7. Return to the heat and bring to the boil, stirring continuously. Cook over a low heat for 2 minutes. Stir in the cheese and egg yolk, season to taste and pour over the meat and aubergines. Top with the breadcrumbs and some extra cheese, if desired.

8. Bake in the oven for 50–60 minutes at 180°C/gas mark 4, until the top begins to brown. If you like a crispy top, put the dish under the grill for a few minutes before serving.

Serving suggestion
Serve with a salad of baby beet and rocket leaves dressed with a little balsamic vinegar.

Strawberry Parfait

A combination of ice cream and sorbet all in one delicious recipe.

Serves 6–8

450g strawberries
250g caster sugar
250ml water
5 egg yolks
350ml double cream

1. Cook the strawberries, sugar and water together in a pan until the fruit is tender. Remove from the heat.

2. Remove the strawberries from the syrup and place in a food processor. Whizz to a purée, then leave to cool.

3. Beat the eggs into the cream and whisk until thick, but not stiff.

4. Drizzle the cool strawberry syrup into the cream and egg mixture and beat continuously.

5. Fold in the strawberry purée. Put the parfait in a freezer-proof container and freeze for 1 hour, then beat.

6. Return it to the freezer and leave for 5 hours before consuming.

Apricot Alaska

Everyone will be amazed at this 'magic' dessert. How does the ice cream not melt in the oven?

Serves 4–6

8 scoops of good-
    quality vanilla
    ice cream

For the sponge
100g butter
100g caster sugar
3 egg yolks
100g self-raising flour

For the fruit topping
7 fresh apricots, halved
    and stoned, stewed
    until tender with a
    tablespoon of golden
    granulated sugar and
    100ml water

For the meringue
3 egg whites
75g icing sugar, plus
    extra for dusting

1. Preheat the oven to 180°C/gas mark 4.

2. Make the sponge by creaming the butter and sugar together. Beat in the egg yolks and fold in the flour. Bake for 15–20 minutes, then allow to cool completely.

3. When you are ready to assemble the Alaska, make the meringue: whisk the egg whites until stiff, then whisk in half the icing sugar. Fold in the rest.

4. Preheat the oven to 220°C/gas mark 7.

5. To assemble the Alaska, place the sponge on an ovenproof pie plate and spoon over the apricots with some of the juice – but not too much, or the sponge will become soggy and difficult to serve. Put the ice cream on top of the apricots and pile the entire dessert with the meringue. Don't smooth it out; leave it looking rough, like snow.

6. Put in a very hot oven for 2–3 minutes, or until the meringue begins to colour. Dust with a little extra icing sugar.

7. Serve immediately with any leftover juice.

Cherry Clafoutis

A wonderfully decadent way to serve gorgeous fresh cherries.

Serves 6

50ml Kirsch (or more
   if you prefer)
400g cherries,
   stones removed
100g plain flour
50g icing sugar
3 eggs, beaten
30g melted butter
300ml milk
Icing sugar, for dusting

1. Pour the Kirsch over the cherries and leave to soak for an hour.

2. Preheat the oven to 220°C/gas mark 7.

3. Combine the flour and icing sugar in a bowl.

4. Add the eggs, butter and milk and whisk together until light and fluffy.

5. Pour a thin layer of the batter into a well-buttered ovenproof dish and bake for 5–7 minutes until set.

6. Put the cherry mixture over the cooked batter, reserving most of the juice.

7. Stir the juice into the remaining batter and pour this over the cherries.

8. Cook for 40–45 minutes at the same temperature as before until well-risen and golden brown. Dust with icing sugar and serve warm with cream.

Cherry Jam

This should keep unopened for six months in a cool, dark place.

Makes 4 x 450g jars

1.5kg cherries
Juice of 2 lemons
1kg sugar
1 x 13g sachet pectin

1. Stone the cherries, reserving a dozen of the stones. Put these in a little muslin bag as this adds flavour to the jam.

2. Put the cherries, lemon juice and stones in a pan and heat to boiling. Turn down the heat and simmer gently for 10 minutes.

3. Take out the bag of stones and squeeze out any juice using tongs.

4. Add the sugar and pectin and stir over a low heat until all the sugar has dissolved.

5. Raise the heat and boil the mixture rapidly for 5 minutes. Test for setting point (see page 19).

6. Cool for 15 minutes. Stir and ladle into sterilised jars, then label and date the jam.

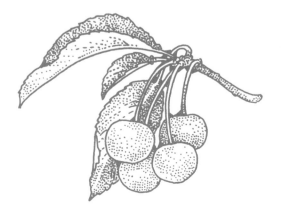

Lemon Balm and Honey Syllabub

A heavenly treat on a warm summer's day. This doesn't set firmly like a mousse, so don't worry if it seems runny. It should be light and 'spoonable', and is delicious served with thin fingers of shortbread.

Serves 6

500ml double cream
80ml pale
   cream sherry
Grated zest and juice
   of 1 lemon
2 dessertspoons
   chopped fresh lemon
   balm leaves
1 dessertspoon honey
1 teaspoon golden
   caster sugar
A few whole lemon
   balm leaves, for
   decoration

1. In a large bowl, whisk all the ingredients together, apart from the reserved leaves, until the mixture thickens but is pourable.

2. Either chill the mixture in a large serving bowl or spoon it into individual glasses and chill. Whichever way you choose, leave for 3 hours before serving with a few lemon balm leaves on top.

We often make the mistake of referring to the high summer of July as 'halcyon days', but they are not. The term *halcyon* comes from Greece via Middle English *hals* ('the sea') and *kuon* ('conceiving'), and referred to the belief that kingfishers flew out to sea to mate. It was thought that they laid their eggs on a specially constructed raft and hoped for fine seas. Consequently, halcyon days in Britain were actually the first days of January, when the sea was flat-calm and no one could find any kingfishers.

Our local river is full of kingfishers; they dart about like blue streaks, and in the riverbanks you can find a season's worth of edible bounty every month of the year. The earliest brambles are not quite ripe in July, but the escapee raspberries from nearby allotments can be picked and turned into new wine, while the borage flowers can be frozen into ice cubes with mint leaves for exclusive Pimms hours in the evening sun on the patio.

July is the time to live off the garden, from now until September, when Indian summer encourages gardeners to plant more salad, radishes and onions. You get the impression of fullness and bounty following all the hard work earlier in spring.

The freshness of the produce in the garden provides an extra sense to eating. We always smell and taste, and it is often said that the 'first bite is with the eye', but texture is so easily overlooked. However, a four-leaf salad in July can include four really different textures, and the combination of sun, good soil and evening moisture produces some of the crispiest lettuce imaginable.

July

July Menu
A three-course meal to serve 4 people

❧

Smoked Salmon Roulade

❧

Beefsteak with Green Beans in a Black Pepper Sauce

❧

Cherry and White Chocolate Gateau

Smoked Salmon Roulade

A simple yet impressive starter that may be served as it is, or with toast fingers or oat cakes.

200g cream cheese
1 tablespoon
  chopped chives
2 tablespoons
  chopped dill
2 teaspoons
  lemon juice
4 slices smoked
  salmon; large slices,
  not narrow strips
Watercress and lemon
  wedges, to serve

1. Mix the cream cheese, herbs and lemon juice together thoroughly.

2. Lay the slices of salmon flat on a worktop or similar flat surface.

3. Spread the cheese mixture evenly over the salmon, spreading as close to the edge as you can.

4. Roll up the salmon as you would a Swiss roll. Trim the edges slightly if they are uneven.

5. Put in the fridge to chill for 30 minutes.

6. Serve each portion sliced on a bed of watercress with lemon wedges.

Beefsteak with Green Beans in a Black Pepper Sauce

A family favourite. Beef and black pepper go so well together, and the crisp beans add texture and interest to the simple sauce.

120g fresh green beans
— dwarf French
are perfect
4 x 150–200g
frying steaks
Salt to taste
1 tablespoon
sunflower oil
20 black peppercorns,
coarsely ground
180ml single cream

1. Steam or boil the beans for 3–4 minutes. Drain and set aside.

2. Season the steaks with a little salt. Heat the oil on a medium heat in a large frying pan and fry the steaks on both sides to your taste (for medium, it's about 4 minutes each side, depending on the thickness of the meat). Remove from the pan and transfer to a warm plate.

3. Put the peppercorns and green beans in the same pan the meat was fried in. Add the cream and stir to remove any juices from the bottom of the pan. Taste to see if the sauce needs salt.

4. Put the steak onto warm serving plates and pour over the sauce, making sure each plate gets its share of green beans.

Serving suggestion
Serve with fried potatoes, thick home-cooked chips or baked potatoes.

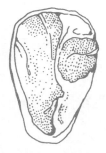

Cherry and White Chocolate Gateau

A very rich and crowd-pleasing dessert.

Serves 6–8

For the sponge
150g butter
150g golden
   caster sugar
150g self-raising flour
3 eggs, beaten
50g white chocolate
   pieces or chips

For the filling
100ml whipping cream
20g white chocolate,
   broken into
   small pieces
20–25 cherries, pitted
   and soaked
   overnight in 4
   tablespoons brandy
   or Kirsch

For the topping
100g white chocolate
15g butter

30g flaked almonds or
   grated chocolate, for
   the top
Fresh cherries for
   decoration – don't
   use soaked ones

To make the sponge
1. Preheat the oven to 180°C/gas mark 4. Grease and line 2 x 20cm sandwich cake tins. (If you use silicone cake 'tins', you don't need to use lining paper, but just grease the tin with a little butter.)

2. Cream the butter and sugar until light and fluffy.

3. Add 1 tablespoon of the flour and beat in the eggs.

4. Sieve in the rest of the flour, then fold it in with the chocolate pieces.

5. Divide the mixture between the two prepared tins.

6. Bake for 20 minutes, or until springy to the touch and golden in colour.

7. Cool for 15 minutes in the tins, then transfer to a wire rack.

To make the filling
1. Whip the cream until firm, but not stiff.

2. Melt the chocolate in a bowl over a pan of very hot water. Fold it into the cream.

To make the topping
Melt the chocolate and butter together in a bowl over a pan of very hot water or in a microwave.

To assemble the cake
1. Put one of the cake sections onto a serving plate and spread with the cream mixture.

2. Squeeze the juice out of the cherries a little as you place them in the cream.

3. Put the second layer of cake carefully on the cherries and spread the top with the melted white chocolate.

4. Sprinkle the top with flaked almonds or grated chocolate and arrange the cherries in the centre, or wherever you think they look attractive.

5. Chill until ready to serve.

Variation
This can be made into the retro recipe of a Black Forest gateau by using 2 tablespoons cocoa powder in the cake mixture, sieved in with the flour and substituting dark chocolate whenever white is used.

Bellini Cocktail

This summery cocktail is ideal to serve with the starter course of a meal.

Serves 6

3 ripe peaches
1 bottle of Champagne
or sparkling
white wine

1. Peel and halve the fruit and remove the stones. Chop into pieces, reserving all the juice.

2. Put the peaches into a food processor and whizz to a smooth purée.

3. Put one-third peach purée to two-thirds Champagne or sparkling wine in each glass. Serve with an ice cube in each glass.

Mangetout and Avocado Salad

A crisp and refreshing salad that is good as a starter or served with grilled mackerel.

Serves 4

400g mangetout,
   trimmed
1 medium avocado,
   peeled and halved,
   stone removed
1 very small
   carrot, grated
2 tablespoons
   lemon juice
2 tablespoons olive oil
1 tablespoon
   clear honey
1 teaspoon chopped
   fresh mint
Salt and pepper
   to taste

1. Blanche the mangetout in boiling water for about 20 seconds. Drain and cool.

2. Chop the avocado into small cubes and place in a bowl.

3. Stir in the mangetout and grated carrot.

4. Whisk the lemon juice, olive oil, honey and mint together and pour over the mangetout mixture.

5. Season with salt and pepper to taste and serve.

Greek-style Salad

Here are lots of fresh tastes to keep your hunger at bay on a hot summer's day. Any firm, creamy-tasting cheese is good in this recipe.

Serves 4–6

1 crushed garlic clove
4 tablespoons olive oil
2 large slices
 wholemeal bread, cut
 into small croutons
Salt and black pepper
 to taste
2 little gem lettuces,
 well washed
1 small (or half a large)
 green pepper, sliced
 into thin strips
Half a small
 cucumber, diced
2 celery sticks, chopped
 into 0.5cm pieces
2 beef tomatoes, sliced
15–20 pitted black olives
120g feta cheese

For the dressing
4 tablespoons olive oil
2 tablespoons
 white-wine vinegar
1 tablespoon
 runny honey
2 pinches dried
 marjoram (or 1
 teaspoon fresh)
Salt to taste

1. Preheat the oven to 220°C/gas mark 7.

2. Put the garlic in the olive oil and stir well. Put the bread on a baking sheet and drizzle with the olive oil. Sprinkle with a little salt and black pepper and mix well together with your hands.

3. Bake for 5–8 minutes, or until golden and crisp. Place on kitchen paper and leave to cool while you prepare the salad.

4. Break up the lettuce into single leaves and place in a large bowl or individual dishes.

5. In another bowl combine the pepper, cucumber and celery and spoon over the lettuce.

6. Put the slices of tomato on top and scatter with the olives.

7. Cube the cheese and add it to the salad. Finish by adding the croutons.

8. Mix all the dressing ingredients together, then use this to dress the salad.

Summer Vegetable Soup

A light yet tasty soup for lunch or as a starter.

Serves 4

50g butter
1 onion, finely chopped
2 carrots, chopped
1 red pepper, chopped
1 medium
  courgette, diced
50g fresh peas
50g green beans, sliced
  into 1cm pieces
Salt and pepper
  to taste
A small handful
  rocket leaves
1 tablespoon chopped
  fresh chives
1 tablespoon chopped
  fresh parsley
1 teaspoon chopped
  fresh mint
1 litre vegetable stock

1. Melt the butter in a large lidded pan and add the next 6 ingredients. Add a pinch of salt and pepper and stir to coat the vegetables in the butter. Turn down the heat.

2. Allow to sweat for 15 minutes, then stir in the rocket and herbs and sweat for 5 more minutes.

3. Add the stock and bring to the boil. Turn down the heat to a simmer and cook for 25 minutes. Serve with bread rolls.

Rabbit Fricassée

A deliciously different way of serving rabbit that could be used for a dinner party.

Serves 4

1 large rabbit, jointed
Salt and pepper
   to taste
1 onion, chopped
1 courgette, sliced
2 carrots, chopped
1 red pepper, chopped
1 tablespoon freshly
   chopped parsley
2 sprigs fresh thyme
1 bay leaf
2 slices wholemeal
   bread, cut into cubes
2 tablespoons olive oil

For the sauce
30g butter
30g flour
175ml of the rabbit
   cooking water
2 tablespoons
   dry sherry
50ml double cream
Salt and pepper
   to taste

1. Put the rabbit into a large pan and pour in sufficient water to cover the meat. Season with salt and pepper. Bring to the boil and simmer for 10 minutes.

2. Add the vegetables and herbs and simmer for 35–40 minutes, or until the rabbit is tender.

3. Pour 175ml of the stock into a jug and put the meat and vegetables in an ovenproof dish.

4. Take all the meat from the bones and discard the bones. Add the meat to the vegetables and keep warm in the oven at about 160°C/gas mark 3.

5. Make the sauce by melting the butter in a pan and stirring in the flour. Add the meat stock gradually over a low heat until it is all combined.

6. Bring to the boil, stirring continuously. Season to taste and cook for 3–4 minutes, then remove from the heat.

7. Stir in the sherry and cream, season to taste and pour the sauce over the rabbit and vegetables.

8. Keep the casserole in the oven while you fry the bread cubes in the oil until crispy.

9. Serve the dish with the croutons, boiled new potatoes and green beans or fresh peas.

Mussels in White Wine and Tomato Sauce

Mussels taste good in this light tomato sauce. Have plenty of chunks of bread on hand to mop up the sauce.

Serves 3–4

30ml sunflower or
   rapeseed oil
1 onion, finely chopped
2 garlic cloves,
   chopped or grated
2 tablespoons
   tomato purée
1 tablespoon chopped
   fresh parsley
100ml white wine
8 small tomatoes,
   chopped
Salt and pepper
   to taste
1.5kg mussels,
   scrubbed; discard
   any that have broken
   shells or don't close
   when tapped
80ml single cream

1. Heat the oil in a large pan and fry the onions with the garlic for 4–5 minutes until soft.

2. Add the tomato purée and parsley.

3. Stir in the white wine and the tomatoes. Season to taste.

4. Bring to the boil and add the mussels all in one go. Cover and cook on a high heat for 5 minutes. Shake the pan gently to allow the mussels to open, but not too vigorously or the shells will break. Stir in the cream.

5. Serve the mussels and sauce in shallow soup dishes.

Variation
To use shelled mussels, use about 400g and add them at stage 4, but cook for 1 minute only.

Summer Vegetable Medley

Try this recipe to make the most of wonderful fresh, seasonal vegetables. Even the meat-eaters shouldn't complain!

Serves 4

400ml vegetable stock
50ml white wine
250g baby carrots,
    trimmed and
    scrubbed
250g fresh or
    frozen peas
250g baby turnips,
    trimmed and washed
1 small head
    cauliflower
    (or half a large one),
    split into florets
100g baby leeks,
    washed and
    sliced in half
100g mushrooms,
    sliced
50g butter
Salt and pepper
    to taste
3 tablespoons
    plain flour
½ teaspoon
    English mustard
1 tablespoon
    double cream
30g breadcrumbs

1. Combine the stock and wine in a large saucepan and bring to simmering point.

2. Add all the vegetables (but not the mushrooms). Cook until tender.

3. Remove from heat, lift out the vegetables and put them in an ovenproof dish. Keep all the liquid. Keep the vegetables warm in a low oven.

4. In another pan, fry the mushrooms gently in the butter and a little seasoning to taste. When soft, turn down the heat and sprinkle in the flour and mustard. Stir into the butter and mushroom liquor.

5. Pour in small amounts of the vegetable stock and stir until it thickens. Add the stock until the mixture has the desired consistency and thickness; you may not wish to add all the stock if you want a very thick sauce. Stir in the cream – this may be omitted if you prefer.

6. Pour the sauce over the cooked vegetables and sprinkle the top with the breadcrumbs.

7. Place the dish under a hot grill to brown the top, and serve with buttered new potatoes.

Summer Pudding

Who doesn't like a summer pudding? The fruity, refreshing taste is combined with the satisfying outer crust that is soaked through with jewel-coloured fruit juice. If you're using any frozen fruit, make sure it's defrosted before heating, otherwise the flavour will be impaired.

Serves 6

8 slices of white bread, preferably at least a day old
800g–1kg soft summer fruits: raspberries, strawberries, redcurrants, whitecurrants, blackcurrants, cherries, etc.
120g caster sugar

1. Butter a 1.1-litre pudding basin. Cut the crusts from the bread and cut a circle from one of the slices to fit the base of the basin. Reserve two slices of bread for the top of the pudding and line the basin with the other slices, slightly overlapping them to form a seal.

2. Put any fresh fruit in a pan with the sugar and heat gently until all the sugar has dissolved. Add any frozen fruit at this point. If using all frozen fruit, put it all in together with the sugar.

3. Heat until simmering and all the juices begin to run. Remove from the heat and allow to cool.

4. Spoon the fruit and juice into the basin until it reaches the top of the rim. Be careful not to disturb the bread. Make a lid to fit the top with the two reserved slices and press down gently, allowing the juice to seep into the bread. Any fruit left over can be served with the pudding.

5. Place a saucer over the pudding and put a can of beans or something heavy on the top to keep it weighed down.

6. Chill in the fridge for 24 hours.

7. Run a knife around the outer edge of the pudding to loosen before turning out onto a plate. Serve with any leftover fruit and cream.

Variation
This can be also made using gooseberries in the fruit mixture, or even with gooseberries on their own; use a little elderflower syrup to flavour the finished pudding.

Raspberry Mousse

This can be made with the amount of double cream in the recipe or half cream and half low-fat crème fraîche for a lighter version.

Serves 6

500g raspberries, fresh
   or frozen and
   defrosted
130g caster sugar
20g powdered gelatine
   dissolved in
   150ml hot water
2 egg whites
280ml double cream

1. Heat the fruit with half of the sugar and simmer for 5 minutes. Allow to cool.

2. Push the fruit through a sieve and stir in the gelatine and extra sugar.

3. Whisk the egg whites until stiff and fold into the fruit mixture.

4. Whisk the cream for a few seconds (but don't allow it to stiffen) and stir into the fruit mixture carefully.

5. Spoon the mousse into glasses and chill for 2 hours. Serve with a raspberry or swirl a little extra cream on top.

Strawberry and Gooseberry Fool Layer

A celebration of the best summer has to offer.

Serves 4 generously

200g fresh
  gooseberries,
  washed, topped
  and tailed
3 tablespoons golden
  granulated sugar
150ml double cream
1 tablespoon
  icing sugar
150ml crème fraîche
8 large strawberries,
  plus a few for
  decoration

1. Put the gooseberries in a pan with the sugar and stew until just soft. Mash some of the fruit down to a pulp, but leave some almost whole. Cool.

2. Combine the cream, icing sugar and crème fraîche and whisk until stiff. When the gooseberries are cool, fold them into the cream mixture.

3. Slice the strawberries lengthways and place a couple of the slices in the bottom of 4 wineglasses.

4. Add a tablespoon of the fool mixture and then a layer of the strawberries. Do this until you are close to the top, finishing with a layer of fool and a slice of strawberry or a whole one for decoration.

5. Chill for 1 hour before serving.

Mascarpone Peaches

Creamy mascarpone cheese is a dream matched with ripe, juicy peaches.

Serves 4

4 large, ripe peaches
150ml marsala wine
1 dessertspoon
   icing sugar
250g mascarpone
   cheese
1 tablespoon
   demerara sugar

1. Peel and halve the peaches and remove the stones. Place them in a saucepan and add the wine. Bring to a simmer and poach very gently for about 10 minutes. Cool.

2. Whisk the icing sugar into the mascarpone.

3. Heat the grill until very hot. Put the peach halves on a baking sheet and put a large spoonful of the mascarpone mixture onto each peach.

4. Sprinkle each peach half with the demerara sugar and grill for about 30 seconds, so that the sugar just begins to melt and 'catch'.

5. Serve immediately with any leftover mascarpone and a glass of marsala wine.

Summer Fruits with Chocolate Dip

The easiest, yet most luxurious dessert worthy of a family party. Have lots of serviettes to hand – this one can get messy!

Serves 6–8

Summer fruits
(strawberries,
raspberries,
gooseberries, slices
of peach and
nectarine, fresh
pineapple pieces,
melon and kiwi-fruit
slices)
100g dark chocolate
100g milk chocolate
100g white chocolate
25g butter
Cocktail sticks, for
dipping the fruit

1. Melt the chocolates and butter together in a large bowl over hot water.

2. Swirl the chocolate together but without mixing too much.

3. Serve the chocolate sauce with the fruit and lots of cocktail sticks.

Variation
Melt the different chocolate types with a little butter in separate bowls and serve.

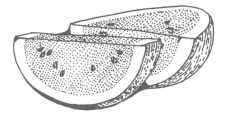

Summer Fruit Jam

This can be made from varying weights of fruit; so long as it all totals up to 2kg it will work well. If you have over half the fruit weight in blackcurrants, don't add any pectin. If no blackcurrants are used, then you'll need a sachet of pectin.

Makes about 3–3.5kg, depending on which fruits are used

2kg fruit: strawberries, raspberries, cherries, blackcurrants and redcurrants
Juice of 1 lemon
1 x 13g sachet of pectin
2kg sugar

1. Wash and prepare the fruit: hull the strawberries and raspberries, top and tail the currants. Remove the cherry stones now, or after cooking if you find it easier.

2. Put all the fruit in a large saucepan or maslin (preserving) pan and heat to simmering.

3. Add the lemon juice and pectin, if using, and keep simmering for 5 minutes, until the juice of the fruit begins to run.

4. Add the sugar and keep simmering until it has dissolved. Stir with a wooden spoon.

5. Bring to the boil and continue to boil until the temperature reaches 105°C if you have a preserving thermometer. If not, test for setting after 4 minutes of boiling time. Have a cold saucer ready and drop half a teaspoon of the preserve onto the saucer; it should cool immediately. Push the jam with your finger, and if the setting point has been reached, it will wrinkle and stay there.

6. Leave to cool for 10 minutes, stir, then ladle into sterilised jars. Seal each jar as you fill it to prevent contamination.

7. Label with the date and flavour of your jam, and store in a cool, dark place. This should keep unopened for at least 12 months. Once opened, it will keep for at least 2 months if stored in the fridge.

Gooseberry Jam

Use firm fruit to make this jam – it gives a better flavour. This jam will keep unopened for at least 12 months if stored in a cool, dark place.

Makes about 3.5–4kg

2kg gooseberries,
  topped and tailed
800ml water
2.5kg sugar

1. Put the gooseberries and water in a saucepan and bring to simmering point. Cook at simmering for about 15–20 minutes, or until some of the skins have broken.

2. Add the sugar and stir until it has all dissolved.

3. Bring to the boil and continue to boil for 8 minutes, then test for setting point (see page 19). Continue to boil if necessary for another 2 minutes, then test again.

4. Leave to cool for 5 minutes, stir and ladle into sterilised jars. Seal immediately, label and date.

Peach and Tomato Chutney

This is a delicious accompaniment to many dishes – cheese tarts and curries are enhanced by its sweet flavour. Try it on a brie and salad sandwich.

Makes approximately 2x 450g jars

12 ripe tomatoes, chopped
5 large peaches, peeled and chopped
2 large red apples, cored and chopped
2 large green apples, cored and chopped
2 large onions, chopped
3 medium stalks of celery, chopped
400ml cider vinegar
250g soft brown sugar
1 level tbsp salt

1. Combine all the ingredients in a large pan over a low heat and stir until the sugar has dissolved.

2. Bring to the boil.

3. Turn down the heat and allow to simmer for 1½–2 hours until the mixture has thickened.

4. Allow to settle and cool for about 10 minutes then ladle into sterile jars and seal well. Label and date the jars.

Strawberry and Apple Jelly

This jelly should keep for six to nine months unopened if stored in a cool, dark place.

Makes 6–7 x 450g jars

2kg strawberries,
   hulled
1kg unpeeled apples,
   cored and diced
750ml water
Sugar: 100g per
   100ml of juice

1. Put the fruit in a large pan with the water and simmer until all the fruit is pulped.

2. Strain the fruit over another pan; do not force the fruit through the sieve as this will cloud the jelly. This could take about 4 hours.

3. Measure the juice and weigh out the appropriate amount of sugar.

4. Warm the sugar in a very low oven for about 5 minutes while heating the juice in a large preserving pan.

5. Pour the sugar into the hot juice and stir over a low heat until the sugar has dissolved.

6. Bring to the boil and boil for 5 minutes. Test for setting point (see page 19).

7. Ladle into the prepared jars and seal. Label and date the preserve.

Sometimes August feels like the first month of autumn. The planet starts its turn away from the sun and moisture rises from the soil. Gardeners spend all the time dead-heading in the hope that this will provide enough blooms to replace the spent ones, but by the time the month is out, they begin to wonder why they bothered.

Somewhere in the middle of the month, the garden, the countryside, wildlife and the produce we eat is at its most mature – as opposed to July when it is at its most perfect. That said, August brings with it the season of fruit, which lasts through to the last apple of November. Plums are a firm favourite; the earliest arrive in late August, which provide wonderful pies, delicious fruit and yet more flavoursome wines and liqueurs.

It is hard to understand why we call the twelfth of the month 'glorious', except that it does have a strong element of seasonality. Hunters, of course, are chomping at the bit to get out there and kill grouse, so by the time the season actually starts, the day seems 'glorious' to them indeed.

Grouse is itself glorious, if a little small. You may feel greedy eating a whole one, but if you do, specialise in the use of your fingers. Many people like their birds hung for a long time, but there are equally as many who do not – and with reason. The action of bacteria on flesh is to putrefy it, so why produce something half-rotten when cooking it can have a healthier, delicious effect?

August

August Menu

A three-course meal to serve 4 people

❧

Rich Tomato and Chilli Soup

❧

Rabbit with Red Peppers

❧

Nectarine Tarte Tatin

Rich Tomato and Chilli Soup

This is an excellent starter course, and very quick and simple to make. You may omit the chilli if you wish.

1 kg ripe tomatoes
50 ml olive oil
2–3 garlic cloves,
   chopped
1 small red chilli
   pepper, chopped
Black pepper to taste
2 anchovy fillets,
   mashed together
1 teaspoon
   brown sugar
Salt to taste

1. Chop the tomatoes roughly.

2. Heat the oil, garlic, chilli, a grind of black pepper and the anchovies together over a low heat. After 2 minutes of stirring, add the tomatoes.

3. Turn up the heat to medium, stir in the sugar and cook for 5 minutes. Remove from the heat and either purée until smooth with a hand blender or put into a food processor.

4. Check for any seasoning adjustments; although the anchovies are salty, it may need a little extra before serving.

Rabbit with Red Peppers

Rabbit and red peppers make perfect partners, and they are both enhanced by the herbs that go into the white-wine sauce of this recipe.

3 tablespoons olive oil
2 onions, sliced
3 garlic cloves, grated
2 large red
  peppers, sliced
2 rabbits, quartered
100ml white wine
250ml chicken or
  vegetable stock
2 teaspoons cornflour
  mixed with 3–4
  teaspoons water
  to make a
  smooth paste
Salt and pepper
  to taste
2 teaspoons thyme
  leaves (or a couple
  of sprigs)
1 bay leaf

1. Preheat the oven to 190°C/gas mark 5.

2. Heat the oil in a frying pan and fry the onions and garlic for 3–4 minutes. Add the peppers. Cook for another couple of minutes and transfer the vegetables to an ovenproof casserole dish.

3. Brown the rabbit portions in the same frying pan and place on top of the vegetables in the dish.

4. Pour the wine and stock into the frying pan and heat until boiling.

5. Add the cornflour mixture, stir well and season to taste. Pour over the rabbit. Add the thyme and bay leaves and stir well.

6. Cover and cook in the oven for about 1 hour, or until the rabbit is tender. Cook for a further 15 minutes if necessary, but don't overcook. Serve with fresh peas and new potatoes.

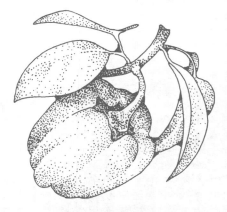

Nectarine Tarte Tatin

This is a summery version of the ever-popular apple tarte tatin – and it is just as delicious.

150g white
  caster sugar
2 teaspoons honey
1 teaspoon lemon juice
3 tablespoons water
50g butter
4–5 nectarines, peeled
  and quartered
250g puff pastry

1. Preheat the oven to 190°C/gas mark 5. Have ready a 22cm nonstick cake tin about 5cm deep.

2. In a sturdy saucepan, add the sugar, honey, lemon juice and water and stir over a low heat until the sugar dissolves,

3. Raise the heat and allow the sugar to turn to caramel brown without stirring. Add the butter and stir quickly. Pour the mixture immediately into the cake tin.

4. Add the quartered fruit to the caramel and bake in the oven for 25–30 minutes.

5. Meanwhile, roll out the pastry until it measures about 30cm square.

6. Use a plate about 4cm in diameter larger than the cake tin and cut a round disc of pastry using the plate as a guide. Prick the pastry all over with a fork.

7. Lift the cake tin out of the oven and press the disc of pastry down onto the fruit. Press firmly around the edges – be careful not to burn yourself! Use the back of a spoon to do this if you prefer.

8. Return the tart to the oven and bake for about 25 minutes, or until the pastry is well-risen and deep golden in colour.

9. Allow the tart to rest for 10 minutes, then loosen around the edges with a knife and place a plate over the top to catch the tart as you turn it over. Serve with cream or crème fraîche.

Pea Soup

August is the season of freshly podded peas, so they are best for this recipe: they give a real taste of summer. But this soup also tastes good made with frozen peas at other times of the year.

Serves 4

30g butter
Half a small onion,
  finely chopped
500g podded peas
  (or frozen, thawed)
800ml vegetable stock
I head little gem
  lettuce, shredded
I teaspoon sugar
Salt and pepper
  to taste
4 tablespoons
  single cream
Mint leaves for garnish

1. Heat the butter in a frying pan and fry the onion gently, until soft.

2. Add the peas and 200ml of the stock. Cook the peas for 5 minutes if using fresh, 2 minutes if using frozen.

3. Add the lettuce and sugar and season to taste with salt and pepper.

4. Cook for 10 minutes at a gentle simmer. Remove from the heat and stir in the cream.

5. Garnish with the mint leaves to serve.

Summer Dips

Served with the spicy pitta bread on the next page, these two dips make a great party starter. They also work well as a dish to go with drinks or cocktails.

Serves 4

Quick Salsa Dip
1 red pepper,
   finely chopped
6 ripe tomatoes,
   chopped
2 shallots or a
   very small onion,
   finely chopped
2 garlic cloves,
   chopped
2 tablespoons sweet
   chilli sauce
2 teaspoons olive oil
A pinch of salt

**Avocado and
Lime Dip**
2 avocados, halved,
   stoned and peeled
2 anchovy fillets
Juice of 2 limes and
   a little zest to
   garnish the dip
300ml crème fraîche
Salt and pepper
   to taste

Quick Salsa Dip
Combine all the ingredients in a bowl and stir well.

Avocado and Lime Dip
1. Put the avocado in a bowl and mash well with a fork.

2. Add the anchovies and lime juice and mash together.

3. Stir in the crème fraîche and season to taste with salt and pepper.

Spiced Pitta Bread Fingers

Spicy pitta bread goes perfectly with most dips, whether you use the ones on the previous page or choose another of your own.

Makes 4 large pittas

300g strong
  white flour
1 teaspoon salt
1 level teaspoon
  cumin seeds
½ teaspoon coriander
  seeds, roughly
  ground
½ teaspoon fennel seeds
1 x 7g sachet
  fast-acting yeast
130ml warm water

1. Sieve the flour and salt together in a bowl. Stir in the spices and yeast.

2. Pour in the warm water and mix to a soft dough. Add more flour or a little extra water if the dough needs adjusting,

3. Knead for 10 minutes to make a smooth dough.

4. Leave to prove for 20 minutes. Preheat the oven to 220°C/ gas mark 7.

5. Dust a little flour onto a work surface and break off a quarter of the dough. Roll it out into an oval shape. Place on an oiled baking sheet and repeat with the rest of the dough.

6. Leave to rest for 10 minutes, then bake for 8–10 minutes, until puffed up and golden.

7. Cool and serve cut into fingers with the dips.

Courgette and Tomato Salad

A winning combination that makes an excellent summery lunch dish.

Serves 4

350g courgettes, sliced
½ teaspoon
   ground cumin
1 tablespoon chopped
   coriander leaves
2 tablespoons
   lemon juice
About 12 mint
   leaves, chopped
3 tablespoons
   virgin olive oil
Salt and pepper
   to taste
250g small
   tomatoes, halved
30g pine nuts
A bunch of watercress

1. Bring a pan of water to the boil containing 1 teaspoon salt and boil the courgettes for 1 minute only. Drain and cool under cold water. Leave to drain completely.

2. Put the cumin, coriander, lemon juice, mint and oil into a bowl and whisk together. Season with salt and pepper and whisk again.

3. Put the courgettes and tomatoes into a serving bowl. Sprinkle with the pine nuts and drizzle with the dressing. Toss everything together.

4. Place some watercress leaves on a plate and spoon the courgette and tomato mixture either on top of or next to the leaves to serve.

Linguine with Crayfish Sauce

The fresh rocket leaves make the ideal accompaniment to this creamy dish.

Serves 4

Linguine: about 120g
    per person, boiled
    in salted water
    according to the
    packet instructions
Parmesan, to serve
Rocket leaves, to serve

For the sauce
30g butter
1 small onion, chopped
1 garlic clove, crushed
2 tablespoons
    tomato purée
1 tablespoon
    chopped dill
2 tablespoons
    lemon juice
15 crayfish tails
200ml fish stock
120ml crème fraîche
Salt and pepper
    to taste

1. First, make the sauce. Melt the butter in a large frying pan and fry the onion and garlic gently until the onion is soft.

2. Add the tomato purée, dill and lemon juice and stir.

3. Raise the heat and add the crayfish tails. Cook for 30 seconds, tossing the crayfish in the sauce.

4. Pour in the stock and bring to the boil. Simmer for 3 minutes and stir in the crème fraîche. Season to taste with salt and pepper.

5. Remove from the heat.

6. Drain the linguine and stir into the sauce.

7. Serve immediately with freshly grated Parmesan and some rocket leaves.

Cheese and Vegetable Crumble

This is delicious and filling on its own, but it could be served with the thick tomato sauce on the next page.

Serves 4

1 medium carrot, diced
50g whole green beans
2–3 green cabbage
   leaves, chopped, or
   4–5 broccoli florets,
   cut in half
1 tablespoon
   sunflower oil
1 onion, chopped
Half a yellow
   pepper, chopped
1 small courgette, sliced
2 garlic cloves, chopped
1 tablespoon
   chopped chives
½ teaspoon thyme
4 medium mushrooms,
   sliced thinly
150g Cheddar or
   similar cheese, grated

For the topping
120g wholemeal flour
Salt and black pepper
   to taste
½ teaspoon
   mustard powder
100g porridge oats
75g butter
Grated cheese

1. Steam the carrots, beans and broccoli (if using) for 3–4 minutes.

2. Heat the oil in a pan and sauté the onions, pepper and courgettes until just soft.

3. Add the garlic, chives and thyme and stir in.

4. Add the mushrooms and cabbage and cook for 3–4 minutes until everything is just cooked.

5. Transfer to an ovenproof dish and sprinkle the cheese over the vegetables.

6. To make the topping: in a mixing bowl, sieve the flour, salt, pepper and mustard together. Stir in the oats.

7. Preheat the oven to 200°C/gas mark 6.

8. Rub in the butter until well mixed, then sprinkle the topping over the vegetables and cheese.

9. Top with a little extra cheese, bake for 30 minutes, then serve.

Rich Tomato Sauce

You can skin the tomatoes if you wish, but the skins add flavour and texture to the sauce. This recipe also makes a good pasta sauce – try adding some fresh basil leaves just before serving.

Serves 4

1 tablespoon olive oil
1 onion, chopped
6 large ripe
   tomatoes, chopped
200ml passata
1 tablespoon
   tomato purée
1 teaspoon
   brown sugar
Salt and black
   pepper to taste

1. Heat the oil in a saucepan and cook the onions gently until translucent. Add the tomatoes and fry until they have 'fallen'.

2. Add the passata, purée and sugar and stir well. Season to taste.

3. Cover and simmer for 10–15 minutes.

Double Gloucester Cheese and Red Onion Tart

This is best served with a green salad and some of the chutneys on the next few pages.

Serves 6

200g shortcrust pastry
100g Double Gloucester
  cheese, grated
2 red onions,
  finely sliced
2 eggs
1 level teaspoon dry
  mustard powder
280ml single cream
Salt and freshly
  ground black
  pepper to taste

1. Grease a 20cm flan tin. Preheat the oven to 200°C/gas mark 6.

2. Roll out the pastry to fit the tin, with a little extra to allow for shrinkage. Line the tin with the pastry, place a sheet of baking paper inside and weigh it down with baking beans. Bake the pastry 'blind' by putting the tin on a baking sheet and baking for 15–20 minutes. The pastry won't be cooked, but it will have set into the correct position to hold the filling. Remove from the oven and set aside.

3. Reduce the oven temperature to 180°C/gas mark 4.

4. Sprinkle half the cheese over the base of the flan and scatter the onion on top. Finish with the rest of the cheese.

5. Beat the eggs, mustard powder and cream together and season to taste. Remember, though, that the cheese is salty. Pour the egg and cream mixture over the cheese.

6. Put back on the baking sheet and bake for 30–35 minutes, or until the egg mixture has set and the top is golden brown.

7. Cool for 10 minutes before slicing.

Tomato Chutney

Use a mixture of green and red tomatoes to add flavour and variety to this recipe if you wish.

Makes about 2kg

200ml malt vinegar
1.5kg tomatoes,
   chopped
1 onion, chopped finely
200g soft brown sugar
1 teaspoon mixed spice
½ teaspoon paprika
2 garlic cloves,
   chopped
2 level teaspoons salt

1. Put half of the vinegar and all the rest of the ingredients into a large, heavy-bottomed pan. Simmer gently until all the sugar has dissolved, stirring all the time.

2. Bring to the boil, then reduce the heat and simmer for 30 minutes, stirring occasionally.

3. Add the rest of the vinegar and cook at simmering for a further 35–40 minutes.

4. Turn up the heat and simmer more vigorously until the chutney thickens – about 5 minutes.

5. Pour into sterilised glass jars and seal immediately. Keep for 7 days before consumption. Once opened, store in the fridge and eat within 4 weeks.

Green Tomato Chutney

When you grow your own tomatoes you inevitably end up at the end of the growing season with some green tomatoes that stubbornly refuse to ripen. Use them in this chutney – it's great with cheese and onion pie.

Makes about 3–3.5kg

1.8kg green tomatoes,
   chopped
700g onions, chopped
2 apples, peeled
   and diced
575ml white vinegar
500g white
   caster sugar
25g chopped fresh
   or ½ teaspoon
   ground ginger
½ level teaspoon
   mixed spice
2 teaspoons salt

1. Put the tomatoes, onions and apples in a large, heavy-based saucepan with half of the vinegar and bring to the boil.

2. Remove from the heat, stir in the sugar and all the other ingredients.

3. Return to a gentler heat. Stir until all the sugar has dissolved and simmer for 30 minutes, then add the rest of the vinegar.

4. Simmer for 1 hour until the chutney thickens, stirring occasionally.

5. Put into sterilised jars and seal immediately. Leave to mature for 2 weeks before consuming.

Quick Tomato Relish

This is a nice and easy recipe you can make and eat within a couple of days. You don't have to make loads at one go, but if you do want to make more, just double the quantities. This is delicious served with burgers and hot dogs, but try it on a sandwich with slices of creamy Brie and salad leaves.

Makes 1 x 450g jar

1 tablespoon olive oil
120g red onions, chopped finely
1 small red chilli, chopped
2 garlic cloves, chopped
½ teaspoon onion seeds
80g soft brown sugar
80ml malt vinegar
½ level teaspoon salt
450g red tomatoes, chopped finely

1. In a large pan, heat the oil gently and fry the onions and chilli together until the onion is soft.

2. Stir in the garlic and onion seeds.

3. Add all the other ingredients and stir well. Bring to the boil, stirring continuously.

4. Turn down the heat to simmering and cook for 50 minutes to 1 hour. The mixture should be thick by this time.

5. Transfer to a sterilised screwtop jar and leave for 24 hours before consuming.

Blackcurrant and Mint Shake

This makes a cooling drink or you can serve it as a dessert on a hot, lazy day.

Serves 4

300g blackcurrants
100ml water
12–15 mint leaves, plus
    extra for garnish
2 level tablespoons
    honey
600ml milk
3 tablespoons
    natural yogurt
4 scoops vanilla
    ice cream

1. Wash the blackcurrants and put them in a pan with the water and mint leaves.

2. Bring to the boil, then simmer for 5 minutes until the currants begin to burst.

3. Push the fruit through a sieve, using a jug or bowl to catch all the juices and pulp that come through.

4. Stir the honey into the juices and allow to cool completely. Chill for 30 minutes in the fridge.

5. Whisk or blend the juices with the milk and yogurt and add the ice cream. Blend in the ice cream and pour into highball-type glasses.

6. Decorate with sprigs of mint before serving. Add a few ice cubes if you want it extra-cold.

Cranachan

This Scottish recipe makes a delightful way to serve raspberries.

Serves 4

50g oatmeal
2 teaspoons
 brown sugar
300ml double cream
30ml clear honey
20ml whisky
350g fresh raspberries

1. Heat the oven to 220°C/gas mark 7 and place the oats on a baking tray. Sprinkle with the sugar.

2. Toast the oats for about 8–10 minutes until golden and remove from the oven. Cool.

3. Whip the cream until it forms soft peaks.

4. Stir in the oats, honey and whisky.

5. Spoon some raspberries into the bottom of 4 large glasses, then stir all but 4 raspberries into the cream mixture.

6. Spoon the cream and oat mixture on top of the raspberries and finish with a raspberry.

7. Chill for 2 hours before serving.

Peach Melba Pudding

A delicious pudding for any occasion. Serve with cream or custard.

Serves 6

3 ripe, fresh peaches
2 tablespoons golden
    caster sugar
A knob of butter
225g raspberries
150g butter
150g golden
    caster sugar
1 egg, beaten
150g self-raising flour

1. Preheat the oven to 180°C/gas mark 4.

2. Place the halved peaches in a frying pan with the sugar and butter and allow the fruit to caramelise slowly over a low heat.

3. Add the raspberries and cook for two more minutes, until the juices begin to run.

4. Place the fruit in a buttered ovenproof dish, making sure the peaches are flat-side down.

5. Meanwhile, cream the butter and the sugar in a bowl and beat in the egg.

6. Sieve the flour into the mixture and gradually fold it in.

7. Spread the mixture carefully over the fruit so as not to disturb it too much and bake for 25–30 minutes.

Yogurt, Raspberry and Redcurrant Dessert

A quick and delicious way to serve redcurrants. You can use white- or blackcurrants instead, or a combination of all three.

Serves 6

300g red, white or
    blackcurrants, plus
    extra to garnish
200g raspberries
80g icing sugar
4 tablespoons
    sweet sherry
50g sponge fingers
350ml natural yogurt

1. Put half of the currants in a bowl and add the raspberries. Cover with half of the sugar and drizzle with the sherry.

2. Crush the other half of the currants with a fork and stir into the fruit mixture.

3. Crush the sponge fingers with a rolling pin and fold into the fruit mixture.

4. Put a spoonful of the fruit mixture into individual serving glasses, then combine the rest of the fruit mixture with the yogurt. Mix well and spoon on top of the fruit layer. Chill for 1 hour.

5. Garnish with a small cluster of currants and serve.

Raspberry Ice Cream

This is a must for a summer evening.

Serves 4–6

400g raspberries
1 teaspoon lemon juice
1 tablespoon icing
  sugar
150ml milk
300ml double cream
3 egg yolks
150g caster sugar

1. Put the raspberries in a bowl and stir in the lemon juice and icing sugar. Mash with a fork, then push through a sieve to purée.

2. Put the milk and cream in a pan and heat on a low heat until very hot.

3. Whisk the eggs and sugar together in a bowl and add the milk mixture. Whisk together and return to the pan.

4. Heat until the custard thickens, stirring all the time. Remove from the heat.

5. Whisk the custard for 1 minute, then fold in the raspberry purée.

6. Put into freezer-proof containers, cover and freeze for 5 hours. Take the ice cream out of the freezer about 10 minutes before serving.

Blackcurrant Jam

Blackcurrant jam has the best flavour. It always remains true to the fresh fruit and, some say, actually tastes better.

Makes 4 x 450g jars

1 kg blackcurrants
500ml water
1.5kg sugar

1. Put the blackcurrants and water in a large pan and bring to the boil. Reduce the heat and simmer for 30 minutes, or until the fruit is tender.

2. Add the sugar and turn down the heat to low while it dissolves. Stir constantly.

3. Bring to the boil and boil rapidly for 5 minutes. Test for setting point (see page 19).

4. Cool for 5 minutes, then stir. Pour into sterilised jars, seal, label and date.

How important the days of September become. Country folk are busy at harvest and market and the seasons usually change mid-month. In days gone by, the harvest meant one thing: landlords required their rent, and the 'quarter day', Michaelmas, was always pay day. In our part of the world, the difficulty of receiving his rent was usually offset by the landlord giving all his tenants a whopping great meal at the Dean Brook on September 29; he collected his rent as everyone filed out.

These days allotments provide cabbages and maincrop potatoes as they did of old, but now we hope for a few extra days of sunshine to ripen the sweetcorn. Where there were once only 'Gardener's Delight' tomatoes, nowadays there are hundreds of varieties, each of them reddening up in the greenhouse. These modern varieties seem to be much better at ripening, and most of the chutney made from them is of the red kind.

September is also the best of months for beachcombing, still warm enough to have a wonderful day out shrimping. Get a big 'T-bar' net and run along the surf. In a remarkably short time you'll have enough for a feast; just be doubly sure there are no sewer outfalls nearby to poison your crop – or you.

September wouldn't be worth the name without fresh fish, caught from the beach and cooked straight away. And eels from off the North Wales coast are so scrummy you'd hardly believe there was any other food in the world.

September

September Menu

A three-course meal to serve 4 people

Wild Mushroom Flamme with Tomato and Onion Salad

Roast Pork with Roasted Butternut Squash and Apple Sauce

Poached Pears with Chocolate Creams

Wild Mushroom Flamme with Tomato and Onion Salad

Probably the easiest tart type dish to make. It is French in origin and can be served with a sweet or savoury filling.

20g butter
150g wild mushrooms
(or a mixture of
2–3 different kinds);
slice the large ones
and halve the
smaller ones
Salt and pepper
to taste
500g puff pastry
150g soft cream
cheese, such as
Philadelphia

1. Preheat the oven to 220°C/gas mark 7.

2. Heat the butter in a saucepan or frying pan and fry the mushrooms until most of the moisture has evaporated. Season to taste, then allow to cool.

3. Roll out the pastry into a square measuring about 30cm x 30cm.

4. Grease a baking sheet very lightly and put the pastry on it. Spread the cheese in the centre, leaving about 4cm around the edge.

5. Spoon the mushrooms evenly over the cheese, making sure you keep the edge free from the filling.

6. Bake for about 25–30 minutes, or until the pastry has risen around the edges and turned deep golden brown.

7. Cool for about 15 minutes before serving with the salad. The flamme can be cut into triangles or squares to serve.

For the salad

4 medium tomatoes,
   sliced into 5 or
   6 pieces
1 red onion,
   thinly sliced
3 tablespoons
   extra-virgin olive oil
3 tablespoons
   cider vinegar
1 teaspoon honey or
   soft brown sugar
Salt and pepper
   to taste
A few basil leaves
   or parsley sprigs
   to garnish

To make the tomato and onion salad

1. Layer the slices of tomato and onion alternately on a serving plate.

2. Whisk the oil, vinegar and sugar or honey together and pour evenly over the tomatoes and onions. Season to taste.

3. Garnished with basil or parsley sprigs and serve with the mushroom flamme.

Roast Pork with Roasted Butternut Squash and Apple Sauce

If you make the apple sauce first, you can then serve it warm or cold with the meat.

1 medium
   butternut squash
Sunflower or olive oil
Salt and pepper
   to taste
The leaves from
   3 thyme sprigs
1.5kg joint of pork
   (boned leg is ideal),
   skin scored well
   with a sharp knife
300ml water
3–4 fresh sage
   leaves, chopped
2 teaspoons cornflour
   or gravy powder
   mixed with 4
   teaspoons cold
   water to make a
   smooth paste

1. Preheat the oven to 200°C/gas mark 6.

2. Peel the squash, halve it and remove the seeds. Cut into 3–4cm chunks and put into a roasting pan. Drizzle with about 2 tablespoons oil and season with salt and pepper to taste.

3. Sprinkle with the thyme leaves and put in the oven to cook at the same time as the meat. During the cooking time, watch to see how the butternut squash is cooking; when it is tender and browned, remove from the oven and place in a warm serving dish. The squash should take about 40–45 minutes.

4. Put the meat joint in a roasting pan, pat dry and season the skin with salt. Pour the water into the bottom of the pan; this helps keep the meat moist and prevents the juices from sticking to the bottom.

5. Put the meat in the oven and cook for 20 minutes. Turn down the heat to 170°C/gas mark 3 and cook for a further 1¼ hours, then test to see if the juices run clear by pushing a skewer into the deepest part of the joint. Cook for a further 15 minutes if necessary.

6. Put the meat on a carving plate and leave to rest for 25 minutes. Pour the juices into a pan and scrape off any bits left on the bottom of the roasting dish. This comes off more easily if you add a little boiling water. Pour this into the other juices.

7. Heat the juices and add the sage leaves. Bring to the boil, adding a little more water if necessary. Stir in enough cornflour/gravy powder mixture to thicken the sauce. Serve in a gravy boat with the meat and squash.

For the apple sauce
 2 Bramley apples,
   peeled and cored
Juice of 1 lemon
2 tablespoons
   caster sugar
4 tablespoons apple
   juice, more if
   necessary
15g butter

For the apple sauce
1. Chop the apples into small pieces and put them in a pan with all the other ingredients except the butter.

2. Bring to the boil. Turn down the heat and simmer for 15–20 minutes until the apples have 'fallen' into the liquid. Add another tablespoon of apple juice if necessary halfway through cooking.

3. Remove from the heat and stir in the butter. Serve as soon as the butter has melted, or cool if you want to serve it cold.

Poached Pears with Chocolate Creams

A variation on a classic dessert. Here, the pears are poached in a combination of sherry and white wine, rather than the traditional red.

For the chocolate creams
2 level tablespoon caster sugar
2 eggs plus 2 egg yolks
400ml double cream
80g dark chocolate, broken into pieces
1 teaspoon cocoa powder, for dusting

For the pears
250ml white wine
50ml pale cream sherry
60g caster sugar
1 tablespoon honey
1 teaspoon vanilla extract
Pinch of cinnamon
4 ripe but still firm pears, peeled but left on the stalks

1. Preheat the oven to 170°C/gas mark 3.

2. Whisk the sugar into the eggs and egg yolks.

3. Heat the cream and chocolate gently together either in a saucepan or the microwave until the chocolate melts; stir very gently to combine.

4. Pour the cream mixture over the egg mixture, whisking gently.

5. Strain the mixture through a fine sieve and pour into individual buttered ramekins.

6. Stand the dishes in a roasting pan with sufficient hot water to come a third of the way up.

7. Cook for about 40–45 minutes, or until they are set. Cool.

8. Dust the tops of the cold chocolate creams with the cocoa before serving with the pears.

For the pears
1. Put everything but the pears into a saucepan and slowly bring to the boil, stirring constantly. Once it boils, turn down the heat to a gentle simmer.

2. Add the pears and poach them in the liquid for about 45 minutes, or until the fruit is translucent.

3. Put the chocolate creams onto a plate next to the pears and serve with a little of the poaching liquid poured over the pears.

Mushroom Soup

A great dinner party recipe. You can vary it by replacing 50ml of stock with 50ml white wine.

Serves 4

50g butter
250g mushrooms,
   chopped
500ml vegetable or
   chicken stock
1 level tablespoon
   plain flour
Salt and black pepper
   to taste
4 tablespoons
   single cream

1. Heat half the butter in a saucepan and fry the mushrooms gently until just soft.

2. Strain the liquor into a measuring jug and add to the stock.

3. Set aside the cooked mushrooms and melt the rest of the butter on a low heat in a saucepan.

4. Stir in the flour with a wooden spoon and gradually add the stock a little at a time. Raise the heat slightly and bring to the boil, stirring constantly.

5. Turn down the heat and simmer gently while adding the mushrooms. Season to taste.

6. Simmer for 2–3 minutes, then add the single cream. Serve immediately with some crusty bread.

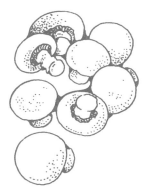

Borscht

If you like beetroot, you'll love this soup. Use rubber gloves if you don't want red hands! You can add lots of freshly ground black pepper to the soup during cooking, but this is optional.

Serves 6

350–400g raw
   beetroot, with
   leaves, washed well
1 tablespoon
   sunflower oil
4 rashers streaky
   bacon, cut into
   small pieces
2 carrots, peeled
   and chopped
1 onion, finely chopped
1.2 litres vegetable
   stock
1 teaspoon
   thyme leaves
1 tablespoon
   red-wine vinegar
Salt and lots of
   black pepper
2–3 tablespoons sour
   cream, to serve

1. Separate the leaves and stalks from the beetroot and chop them finely. Peel the beetroot itself, then chop into dice or thin slices.

2. Heat the oil in a large pan over a medium heat and add the bacon. Fry until the fat runs, then add the chopped beetroot, carrots and onions. Cook until the onions are soft.

3. Stir in the stock, thyme and vinegar and season to taste. Bring to the boil, then turn down the heat and simmer for 30 minutes.

4. Remove from the heat and blend to a thick purée, or hand blend roughly to leave chunks of vegetables.

5. Serve with a swirl of sour cream.

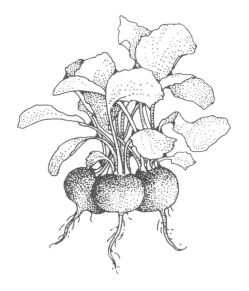

Baked Stuffed Marrow

An old favourite that never fails to please.

Serves 4

1 medium marrow
50g butter
1 onion, chopped
3 ripe tomatoes,
 chopped
100g mushrooms,
 chopped or sliced
2 garlic cloves,
 chopped
50g strong-flavoured
 cheese, such as
 mature Cheddar
 or white Stilton
50g breadcrumbs
Salt and pepper
 to taste

1. Cut the marrow in two lengthways, three-quarters of the way up instead of exactly in half. Scoop out the seeds so that you have a larger channel in which to hold the stuffing. The marrow should now have a boat shape.

2. Heat half of the butter in a saucepan or frying pan and fry the onion for 2–3 minutes, then add the tomatoes, mushrooms and garlic. Cook for 5 minutes on a low heat.

3. Put the mushroom mixture in a bowl and add the cheese and breadcrumbs. Season and stir well. Preheat the oven to 180°C/ gas mark 4.

4. Fill the inside of the marrow with the filling and dot with the remaining butter.

5. Put in a roasting pan and cover with foil. Bake for 50 minutes to 1 hour.

Variation
For a crispier topping, put just the mushroom filling into the marrow, then sprinkle the breadcrumbs and cheese mixture on top.

Roast Duck with Blackberry Sauce

A wonderful meal when served with creamy mashed potatoes and buttered carrots.

Serves 2–3

1 x 1.5kg prepared duck
Juice of 1 lemon
A little oil
Salt and pepper
   to taste
300ml poultry stock
2 tablespoons
   plain flour

For the sauce
200g blackberries,
   washed and hulled
150ml red wine
2 tablespoons
   caster sugar
25g butter

1. Preheat the oven to 200°C/gas mark 6.

2. Put the duck on a rack inside a roasting pan. Sprinkle the lemon juice inside the bird.

3. Prick the breast and legs well with a fork and rub in a little oil. Season with salt and a little pepper, then roast in the oven for about 1¾ hours.

4. Meanwhile, make the sauce. Put the blackberries in a pan with the wine and sugar. Simmer until the fruit is soft and the juice is running.

5. Pass the mixture through a sieve, pushing as much of the pulp through as you can.

6. Return to the pan and heat with the butter, until the butter melts into the sauce. Stir.

7. When the duck is cooked, remove from the pan and place on a carving plate. Pour the fat into a jug and use to roast potatoes.

8. Allow the duck to rest for about 15 minutes, then carve the meat and serve with the sauce.

Three Fish Pie

A wonderful taste of the seaside that is perfectly partnered by garden peas or broccoli.

Serves 6

200g cod fillet (or
   other white fish)
150g natural smoked
   haddock
500ml milk
100ml white wine
50g butter
1 leek, sliced
150g scallops
2 level tablespoons
   plain flour
2 tablespoons fresh
   chopped parsley
Salt and pepper
   to taste
5 medium potatoes,
   peeled, boiled and
   mashed with some
   salt and pepper
   to taste
100g grated Cheddar

1. Put the cod and haddock together in a saucepan with the milk and wine and simmer gently for 10 minutes. Remove the fish from the milk and reserve the poaching liquid. Flake the fish in a bowl.

2. Melt the butter in a pan and fry the leeks until soft. Fry the scallops on both sides while the leeks are cooking, then transfer just the scallops to an ovenproof dish.

3. Gradually stir the flour into the butter and leeks and gradually stir in the poaching liquid.

4. Add the parsley and season with salt and pepper to taste. Cook for 2–3 minutes, stirring constantly, until the mixture thickens.

5. Add the flaked fish and cook gently together for a minute. Pour into the dish with the scallops and stir together. Allow to cool for 15 minutes.

6. Preheat the oven to 190°C/gas mark 5.

7. Spoon the mashed potato over the fish and top with the grated cheese.

8. Bake in the oven for about 30–35 minutes, or until the top is golden.

Bacon and Mushroom Tortellini

This dish uses tortellini, but any shape of pasta will do. The same goes for the mushrooms – just use any type you like that is available.

Serves 4

1 tablespoon olive oil
4 bacon rashers,
   chopped
100g mushrooms,
   sliced
1 garlic clove, grated
500g tortellini
1 tub crème fraîche
Salt and pepper
   to taste
50g Parmesan, grated

1. Preheat the oven to 190°C/gas mark 5.

2. Heat the olive oil in a saucepan or frying pan and fry the bacon, mushrooms and garlic together.

3. Boil the tortellini as per the packet instructions in salted water and drain. Put back in the pan and stir in the cooked bacon and mushrooms. Add the crème fraîche and season to taste.

4. Put the mixture into an ovenproof dish and sprinkle with the cheese.

5. Bake for 15 minutes until the cheese melts and bubbles. Serve with a crispy green salad.

Apple Pie with Cheddar Crust

This is a real tasty twist on the good old apple pie. Serve this with a mixture of cream and crème fraîche; custard just doesn't quite taste right.

Makes 6–8 portions

For the pastry
120g plain white flour
100g wholemeal flour
½ level teaspoon
   salt, optional
50g butter and 60g
   lard, both fats cut
   into cubes and
   chilled until needed
100g mature
   Cheddar, grated
Water to make
   a dough

For the filling
3 Bramley apples
1 tablespoon
   lemon juice
3 tablespoons soft
   brown sugar
50ml water

1. To make the pastry, sieve the flours (and the salt if using) together into a large mixing bowl.

2. Rub in the chilled fats until the mixture looks like breadcrumbs.

3. Stir in the cheese.

4. Add 2 tablespoons cold water and stir in with a knife. Combine the mixture lightly with the fingers; add an extra teaspoon of water if the mixture is too dry. The dough must be soft but not sticky.

5. Chill for 20 minutes.

6. Preheat the oven to 190°C/gas mark 5. Grease a 20cm pie dish. Roll out two-thirds of the pastry to fit the pie dish.

7. Peel, core and slice the apples. To use them uncooked, drizzle them with lemon juice and put into the pastry shell without prior cooking. Sprinkle them with the brown sugar. If you prefer using cooked apples, put them in the pan with the lemon juice, water and sugar and bring to the boil. Turn down the heat and simmer for 5 minutes. Allow to cool before spooning over the pastry shell.

8. Top the pie with the last portion of pastry, rolling it out just until it fits the top. Moisten the edges and press together to seal.

9. Make 2 slits in the centre of the pastry lid to allow the steam to escape.

10. Bake for 35–40 minutes, or until the pastry is deep golden in colour. Serve hot or cold.

Blackberry Mousse

A fruity, fresh-tasting mousse that can also be served in four individual ramekin dishes if you prefer.

Serves 4

450g blackberries,
   washed and hulled;
   reserve a few whole
   berries for garnish
100g caster sugar
11g powdered gelatine
3 tablespoons
   tepid water
150 ml double cream
2 egg whites

1. Put the blackberries in a pan with the sugar over a low heat until the juice of the blackberries runs freely.

2. Put the gelatine in a bowl and stir in the water. Stir the gelatine into the blackberries and remove from the heat.

3. Push the blackberry mixture through a sieve and leave to cool.

4. Whip the cream until it forms soft peaks.

5. In another bowl, whisk the egg whites until they form soft peaks also.

6. When the blackberry mixture is cool, fold the cream into the fruit mixture and then fold in the egg whites.

7. Transfer to a serving dish or mould and chill for 2 hours, or until set. The mousse can be removed from the mould or dish by either running it under warm water or running a knife around the rim of the mould and turning it onto a serving plate.

8. Serve with some fresh blackberries to garnish.

Nutty Plum and Damson Crumble

This is a wonderful late summer or early autumn combination.

Serves 6

300g plums, halved
and stoned
200g damsons, stoned
80g demerara sugar
220g plain flour
½ teaspoon mixed spice
130g butter
50g chopped hazelnuts
140g soft brown sugar

1. Preheat the oven to 200°C/gas mark 6.

2. Put the prepared fruit onto a baking sheet and sprinkle with the demerara sugar. Bake for 20 minutes, or until the fruit has softened and the sugar has begun to caramelise.

3. Transfer the fruit to an ovenproof dish. Turn the heat down to 190°C/gas mark 5.

4. Sieve the flour and mixed spice together into a large bowl and rub in the butter until the mixture looks like breadcrumbs. Stir in the nuts and brown sugar.

5. Sprinkle the mixture over the fruit and bake for 25–30 minutes, or until the top is golden brown.

6. Serve hot or cold with custard, cream or ice cream.

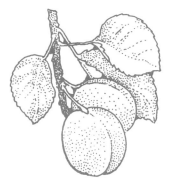

Runner Bean Chutney

A great recipe to use if you have any runner beans that have become too big and may be slightly tough.

Makes 4 x 450g jars

1kg runner beans,
   chopped into
   1cm pieces
700g onions, chopped
700g soft brown sugar
700ml white vinegar
½ teaspoon salt
1 teaspoon turmeric
1 teaspoon
   ground cumin
½ teaspoon
   mustard powder

1. Put the beans in a large saucepan with just enough salted water to cover them. Simmer until tender.

2. In a separate pan, add the onions, sugar, vinegar, salt and spices and heat gently, stirring until the sugar has dissolved. Bring to the boil and cook at boiling for 20 minutes.

3. Meanwhile, drain the beans and add them to the onion and vinegar mixture. Boil for 10 minutes, or until the mixture thickens.

4. Ladle the preserve into sterile screwtop jars, seal and label. Leave to mature for 3–4 days before consuming.

Plum Jam

If you use the freshest English plums, you won't need to add pectin. Use any others and you will need to add about 7g pectin with the sugar in this recipe. This will keep for up to one year unopened.

Makes 5 x 450g jars

1.5kg Victoria or
    other English plums,
    stoned and halved
280ml water
1.5kg sugar

1. If you don't want large pieces of fruit in your jam, cut the plums into chunks.

2. Put the fruit in a saucepan with the water and simmer until the liquid has reduced by half. This will take about 15–20 minutes.

3. Add the sugar and stir until it has dissolved completely.

4. Bring to the boil and cook at boiling for 6–8 minutes.

5. Test for setting point (see page 19) and leave for 5 minutes to cool, then stir and pot in sterilised jars. Label and date when cool.

Redcurrant Jelly

Makes 6 x 450g jars

2kg redcurrants
600ml water
Sugar: 80g per
   100ml of juice

1. Put the fruit in a pan with the water and simmer for 25–30 minutes, or until the currants are tender. Mash the fruit while it cooks to help release the juice.

2. Strain through a jelly bag for 4–5 hours, or until it stops dripping from the bag.

3. Measure the juice and weigh out the necessary amount of sugar.

4. Put the juice and sugar together in a large saucepan and heat gently, stirring constantly until the sugar has dissolved.

5. Bring to the boil and boil rapidly for 10 minutes, then check for setting point (see page 19).

6. Skim the froth from the top if necessary, then stir, pot into sterilised jars, label and date.

Elderberry Cordial

When picking elderberries, do so on a dry day, as the fruit will be fresher-tasting and juicier. Have a large two-litre jug ready to measure the juice yield. The cordial can be diluted one part cordial to four parts water.

Makes at least 1 litre

2kg elderberries
Water to just cover
   the fruit
White granulated
   sugar: 350g for
   every 500ml
Cloves and nutmeg,
   if required

1. Wash the elderberries but don't remove the stalks. Put them in a large saucepan with just enough water to cover the fruit.

2. Heat to simmering and continue to simmer gently for 2–3 minutes. Do not allow the mixture to boil at this stage. Remove from the heat.

3. Strain the liquid into a measuring jug and measure how much the fruit has produced. Weigh out the sugar.

4. Put the juice, sugar and spices, if using, in a pan and heat gently until the sugar has dissolved, then boil for 5 minutes.

5. Cool and decant into sterilised bottles.

October could almost be called apple month, and around the country it is always a time of preparation. It is interesting that there are more varieties of apples in the world than almost any other plant, except for blackberries and raspberries.

Apples have to be collected, cleaned and stored in such a way that they do not deteriorate; a well-stored apple will last into February. Usually, they're wrapped in tissue and stored so that plenty of air circulates around each fruit, but our favourite way of 'storing' them is within the crust of an apple pie. This is the time of year to make many and layer the freezer with luxurious sweets.

Until recently, October was also a time of preparation. The big freeze of 1963 saw people stockpiling tinned food in October, and it was a good job they did. From November to February during that year, times were really hard, even in the centre of a big city.

People who make and prepare their own food know October always means hard work, but they also know that all the effort is worth it. Making preserves at this time of the year creates new foods that are perfect reminders of the sunshine (or otherwise) of the summer. And finally, there is perfection to be had, especially when you press the last drop of juice from the thousands of apples, and make granola from the pulp.

October

October Menu
A three-course meal to serve 4 people

❧

Pumpkin Soup

❧

Pheasant Pot Roast with Root Vegetables

❧

Blackberry and Apple Amber

Pumpkin Soup

Pumpkins and October are practically inseparable, so here is a truly seasonal soup.

1 pumpkin, weighing about 800g–1kg, deseeded, peeled and cut into 3–4cm chunks
2 tablespoons sunflower oil
20g butter
1 large onion, chopped
2 medium potatoes, peeled and cut into cubes
1 teaspoon mild curry powder
1 teaspoon thyme leaves
Salt and black pepper to taste
1 litre vegetable stock
200ml milk
100ml single cream, at room temperature before adding to the soup

1. Preheat the oven to 220°C/gas mark 7.

2. Put the pumpkin chunks on an oiled baking sheet. Drizzle it with the oil and roast for 20–25 minutes, or until they begin to brown and become tender.

3. While the pumpkin cooks, melt the butter in a large pan and fry the onions for 3–4 minutes.

4. Add the potatoes, curry powder and thyme and season with salt and pepper. Cook over a gentle heat for 10 minutes.

5. Pour in the stock and milk and bring to the boil. Turn down the heat and simmer for 5 minutes.

6. Add the roasted pumpkin and cook for another 5–6 minutes.

7. Remove from the heat and blend or mash the soup to as smooth a texture as you prefer.

8. Return to the heat if necessary and swirl in the cream to serve.

Pheasant Pot Roast with Root Vegetables

This recipe is ideal for cooking both young or more mature birds.

6 rashers streaky bacon
2 prepared pheasants
50g butter
2 tablespoons
 sunflower oil
2 large carrots, cut
 into batons
1 turnip, peeled and
 cut into batons
Half a small swede,
 peeled and cut
 into batons
2 tablespoons brandy
200ml poultry or
 game stock
15g butter mixed with
 15g plain flour
 (knead or mix
 this together)
Salt and pepper
 to taste

1. Preheat the oven to 180°C/gas mark 4.

2. Tie 3 rashers of bacon around the breast of each bird.

3. Melt the butter in a large frying pan, mix in the oil and brown the pheasants all over. Put them in a large lidded casserole.

4. Add the vegetables, arranging them evenly around the pheasants.

5. Put the brandy and stock into the frying pan to heat to boiling, then add the butter and flour mixture to thicken the sauce. Pour over the pheasants and vegetables and season to taste with salt and pepper.

6. Put on the lid and cook in the oven for about 1½ hours, or until tender.

7. Serve the pheasant, half a bird per person, with the vegetables and some creamed potatoes.

Blackberry and Apple Amber

This was a wartime favourite because you could make it very successfully with reconstituted dried eggs, but it is even more delicious made with fresh! This is best eaten immediately with cream or vanilla ice cream.

1 large Bramley apple, peeled, cored and sliced
200g blackberries, washed and hulled
2 tablespoons caster sugar
4 tablespoons water or apple juice
50g fresh breadcrumbs
2 large eggs
150ml milk

1. Preheat the oven to 170°C/gas mark 3.

2. Stew the apples and blackberries together with the sugar and the water or apple juice for 8–10 minutes, until the fruit begins to 'fall'.

3. Add the breadcrumbs to the cooked fruit.

4. Whisk the eggs and milk together and stir into the apple mixture.

5. Transfer the mixture to a buttered ovenproof dish and bake for 35–40 minutes until firm.

Autumn Vegetable Soup

A delicious way to make the most of the seasonal harvest.

Serves 4

50g butter
1 large onion, chopped
3 carrots, chopped
350g celeriac, peeled
    and chopped
3 fresh sage leaves,
    chopped
1 litre vegetable stock
8 large mushrooms,
    sliced or chopped
150g marrow
    flesh, cubed
1 tablespoon chopped
    fresh parsley
Salt and pepper
    to taste
Grated cheese of
    your choice, for
    sprinkling (optional)

1. Melt the butter in a large pan and add the onions. Cook over a low heat for 3–4 minutes.

2. Add the carrots, celeriac and sage. Cover and allow the vegetables to sweat in the butter for about 10 minutes.

3. Pour in the stock and stir well. Bring to the boil, then turn down the heat and simmer for 10 minutes.

4. Add the mushrooms, marrow and parsley, season to taste and cook for a further 15 minutes.

5. Serve with fresh bread and sprinkle the top with grated cheese if you wish.

Pork and Apple Cottage Pie

A tasty and economical dish that goes well with green beans or broccoli.

Serves 4

1 tablespoon sunflower
or similar oil
1 medium onion,
finely chopped
1 garlic clove, chopped
500g lean minced pork
2 rashers bacon,
chopped
Salt and pepper
to taste
Water
½ teaspoon dried sage
1 Bramley or 2
dessert apples,
peeled and chopped
1kg potatoes, peeled
and cut into chunks
20g butter
1 teaspoon
English mustard

1. Heat the oil in a saucepan or deep frying pan and fry the onion and garlic until soft but not brown.

2. Add the meat and bacon and fry until it changes colour.

3. Season with salt and pepper and add just enough water to cover the meat mixture. Stir in the sage and simmer for 30 minutes.

4. Add the apples and simmer for 15 minutes. If there is a lot of liquid, you may wish to thicken it with a little cornflour and water mixed together and stirred in well. Put the meat mixture into an ovenproof dish.

5. Preheat the oven to 200°C/gas mark 6.

6. Boil the potatoes until tender and drain well. Season to taste, then add the butter and mustard. Mash well and spoon on top of the meat mixture. Use a fork to make peaks in the potato.

7. Bake for about 20 minutes, or until the potato begins to brown. Cook for 15 minutes extra if the meat was cold when the potato topping was put on.

Mackerel Fillets in Oatmeal

This is a great way to fry mackerel, as the oatmeal goes crispy and tastes amazing with the fish.

Serves 4

8 medium-sized
   mackerel fillets
Salt and pepper
   to taste
100g coarse oatmeal
80g butter or
   bacon fat
1 tablespoon
   chopped parsley
1 lemon sliced

1. Season the fish with salt and pepper. Put the oatmeal on a plate.

2. Roll the fish in the oatmeal. Coat well; it will stick as the fish is oily.

3. Heat the butter or bacon fat in a large frying pan until it sizzles. Fry the fish for about 3 minutes on both sides.

4. When crispy, serve sprinkled with parsley and the lemon slices. Some simple bread and butter is ideal with this dish.

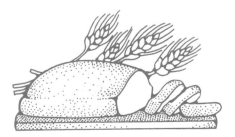

Pasta with Walnut Pesto Sauce

A delicious variation on Italian basil pesto, this recipe still contains pine nuts because they add to the texture of the finished sauce. You do need a food processor to make this successfully.

Serves 4

2 garlic cloves, peeled
50g walnuts, whole or
  chopped roughly
1 tablespoon fresh
  chopped parsley
30g pine nuts
30g freshly grated
  Parmesan, plus
  extra to serve
Salt and pepper
  to taste
100ml olive oil
400g pasta of
  your choice

1. Put the garlic, walnuts, parsley and pine nuts into a food processor and whizz until the mixture looks fairly smooth.

2. Add the Parmesan and any seasoning and whizz again.

3. While the motor is running, gradually add the olive oil until the mixture is a thick paste. You don't need to add all the oil if the mixture is thick and smooth.

4. Cook the pasta in plenty of boiling water with salt added to taste according to the packet instructions.

5. Drain the pasta, put back into the hot pan and stir in the pesto sauce. Serve in pasta bowls with a little extra grated Parmesan on top.

Vegetable Chilli

The addition of bulgur wheat makes this a very filling meal on cold, misty days. Serve it with baked potatoes, boiled rice or simply some good crusty bread.

Serves 4

Oil for frying
1 large onion, chopped
300g pumpkin or
  squash, cut into
  small cubes
2 carrots, diced
2 sticks celery,
  chopped
3 tablespoons
  tomato purée
1 x 400g can plum
  tomatoes or 6
  very ripe fresh
  tomatoes, chopped
2 garlic cloves, grated
1 teaspoon
  chilli powder
1 level teaspoon
  ground cumin
½ teaspoon paprika
2 tablespoons coarse
  bulgur wheat
Salt to taste
50g mushrooms, sliced
1 teaspoon
  brown sugar
1 x 400g can red
  kidney beans,
  drained

1. Heat the oil in a large pan and gently fry the onions for a few minutes until tender.

2. Add the pumpkin or squash, carrot, celery, tomato purée and fresh tomatoes if using them and a couple of tablespoons of water. Stir in the garlic and spices and cook for 3–4 minutes.

3. Stir in the plum tomatoes if you are using them, and add the bulgur wheat. Season to taste and simmer gently for 20 minutes.

4. Add the mushrooms, brown sugar and beans and continue to cook for a further 10 minutes, then serve.

Danish Apple Cake

This can be served hot with cream or custard, or sliced cold as a teatime treat.

Makes 8 portions

150g butter
150g golden
  caster sugar
150g self-raising flour
2 eggs
25g ground almonds
30g sultanas
3 dessert apples,
  peeled, cored
  and sliced
2 tablespoons soft
  brown sugar
  mixed with
  2 level teaspoons
  ground cinnamon
20g flaked almonds

1. Preheat the oven to 180°C/gas mark 4. Butter a 20cm cake tin.

2. Cream the butter and sugar together in a mixing bowl.

3. Add 1 tablespoon flour and beat in the eggs.

4. Fold in the flour and ground almonds and stir in the sultanas.

5. Put half the cake mixture in the tin and smooth out the top. Put a layer of the apples over the top and sprinkle with half of the sugar and cinnamon mixture.

6. Spoon the rest of the cake mixture over the apples and top with rest of the apples. Sprinkle with the rest of the sugar and cinnamon mixture.

7. Spread the flaked almonds evenly over the top.

8. Bake for 40–45 minutes, or until the cake is firm yet springy to the touch.

9. Cool in the tin for 10 minutes before transferring to a serving plate if being served hot. If not, transfer to a cooling rack. Store in an airtight tin.

Caramelised Apples and Pears in Calvados

Serve this decadent dessert with double cream or vanilla ice cream.

Serves 4

30g butter
4 tablespoons golden
  caster sugar
3 dessert apples,
  peeled, cored and
  sliced or cut
  into rings
2 large ripe pears,
  peeled, cored
  and quartered
4–5 tablespoons
  Calvados

1. In a sturdy frying pan, melt the butter and sugar together over a low heat.

2. When the mixture begins to boil, add the apple and pears. **Be careful: the sugary mixture will be very hot and can cause painful burns if it splashes the skin.**

3. Boil for 1 minute, then turn down the heat and simmer for 2–3 minutes. Remove from the heat, and allow to cool for a few seconds.

4. Add the Calvados carefully and stir without breaking up the apples. Serve immediately.

Ginger, Pear and Walnut Muffins with Ginger Cream

Pears and walnuts are such great natural partners, and the ginger cream only enhances their flavour.

Makes 12–15

200g self-raising flour
¼ teaspoon
   ground cinnamon
60g golden
   caster sugar
2 eggs, beaten
100g butter, melted
2 tablespoons milk
1 teaspoon grated
   root ginger
200g pears, peeled,
   cored and chopped
50g chopped walnuts

1. Preheat the oven to 190°C/gas mark 5. Put paper muffin cases in a muffin tin.

2. Sift the flour and cinnamon together into a mixing bowl and stir in the sugar.

3. Make a well in the flour and add the eggs, melted butter, milk and ginger. Mix well with a fork.

4. Gently stir in the pears and walnuts.

5. Spoon the mixture into the paper cases until they reach about two-thirds up each case.

6. Bake for about 20 minutes, or until well risen and springy to the touch.

7. Cool on a wire rack for 5 minutes and serve warm with the ginger cream.

For the ginger cream
Mix ½ teaspoon ground ginger, a pinch ground cinnamon and 1 tablespoon honey into 150ml double cream. Whisk for a few seconds to combine everything and serve.

Stuffed Baked Apples

Marzipan in the dried-fruit stuffing makes these apples an extra-special treat.

Serves 4

4 Bramley apples,
  cores removed
50g soft brown sugar
50g mixed dried fruit
60g marzipan, cut into
  small pieces
2 tablespoons honey
A knob of butter for
  each apple
Double cream,
  to serve
1 tablespoon rum,
  to serve

1. Preheat the oven to 180°C/gas mark 4. Butter an ovenproof dish.

2. Put the apples in the dish.

3. Combine the dried fruit and marzipan and push down into the cavity of each apple. Fill each apple generously.

4. Drizzle the honey down through the centre of the apples over the filling. Put a knob of butter on top of each apple.

5. Bake in the oven for 40–45 minutes and serve with double cream laced with a tablespoon of rum.

Sticky Gingerbread

To vary this recipe, add 50g of raisins or sultanas to the dry ingredients before adding the melted butter. If you really like ginger, use 25g chopped ginger in syrup as well as the ground ginger. Drain away any syrup before stirring into the melted butter.

Makes 16 squares

225g self-raising flour
1 teaspoon ground
    ginger
110g soft brown sugar
120g butter
1 tablespoon
    golden syrup
2 egg yolks – reserve
    the whites for
    the topping
2 egg whites
    (see above)
2 tablespoons
    demerara sugar

1. Preheat the oven to 170°C/gas mark 3. Grease a rectangular 18cm x 10cm tin.

2. Sieve the flour and ginger together into a large mixing bowl and stir in the sugar.

3. Melt the butter and syrup together in a pan over a gentle heat. As soon as the butter has melted, remove from the heat and stir in the egg yolks.

4. Pour the butter mixture into the flour and stir well to combine all the ingredients.

5. Put the sticky dough into the prepared tin and press down well.

6. Brush the top of the dough with the egg white and sprinkle with the demerara sugar.

7. Bake for 30–35 minutes. Cool for 15 minutes, then cut into squares. Leave in an airtight tin for 24 hours before consuming.

Bramley Jam

A must for this time of year, when Bramleys are at their best. Halve the quantities if you want to make less. This should keep unopened for up to a year. Once opened, store in the fridge and use within six weeks.

**Makes about
10 x 450g jars**

3kg Bramley apples
1 litre water
4 tablespoons
   lemon juice
3kg sugar
1 level teaspoon
   ground cinnamon

1. Halve and core the apples; you don't need to peel them but do so if you prefer. Put the cores and any peelings in a muslin bag and tie it securely.

2. Slice or dice the apples and put them in a pan with the water and lemon juice.

3. Add the muslin bag containing the cores and peel (if there is any) and bring it to the boil. Turn the heat down and simmer until the apples start to pulp. Remove from the heat.

4. Add the sugar and cinnamon and stir in well. Put the pan back on a low heat and stir until the sugar has dissolved.

5. Raise the heat and bring everything to the boil.

6. Boil rapidly for 5 minutes, then test for a setting point (see page 19).

7. Allow the jam to cool for 5 minutes, then ladle it into sterilised jars. Label and date.

Mincemeat

This wonderful mincemeat is best made about six to eight weeks in advance to allow the flavours to develop fully. It will keep for four to five months in a cool, dark place.

Makes 4–5 x 450g jars

450g cooking apples,
  cored and diced
225g vegetarian suet
280g soft brown sugar
1kg mixed dried fruit,
  raisins, sultanas
  and currants
110g glacé
  cherries, halved
½ teaspoon mixed spice
½ teaspoon cinnamon
½ teaspoon
  grated nutmeg
Juice and zest
  of 1 lemon
5 tablespoons brandy

1. Stew the apples on a low heat until tender. Leave to cool.

2. Meanwhile, mix all the other ingredients together in a big bowl, making sure everything is well-coated in the brandy.

3. When the apples are cool, mix them well into the other ingredients.

4. Pack into sterilised jars and seal well. Mature for at least 2 weeks before using.

Autumn Chutney

This uses autumnal fruits and is a delicious accompaniment to pork pies and creamy cheeses. You can use any amount of each fruit so long as the total weight is 1.5kg – there is no 'rule' as to how much of each fruit you need.

Makes 4–5 x 450g jars

1.5kg in total of apples, pears and plums, cored, stoned and chopped into small cubes
80g chopped dates
100g raisins
450g onions, finely chopped
2 garlic cloves, chopped
350g soft brown sugar
550ml malt vinegar
1 level teaspoon allspice
1 level teaspoon ground ginger
½ teaspoon white pepper
1 rounded teaspoon salt

1. Put all the ingredients into a large pan over a gentle heat. Stir while all the sugar dissolves.

2. Bring to the boil, then turn down the heat and simmer for 1½ hours until the mixture has thickened and turned glossy. Stir a couple of times during the cooking process.

3. Pot immediately in sterilised jars. Label and date. Leave to mature for 1 week in a cool, dark place.

Tomato and Pumpkin Chutney

This combination is perfect as a winter pick-me-up. It's especially delicious when served with cheese and cold ham.

Makes about 2–2.5kg

1kg pumpkin flesh, cut
    into 1.5cm cubes
500g red tomatoes,
    chopped
300g onions,
    chopped finely
50g raisins
50g sultanas
750g brown sugar
580ml white vinegar
2 level teaspoon
    ground ginger
1 level teaspoon
    ground cinnamon
1 level teaspoon
    ground black pepper
2 garlic cloves,
    chopped
2 level tablespoons salt

1. Put all the ingredients into a large pan over a low heat. Stir until all the sugar has dissolved.

2. Turn up the heat and bring to the boil, stirring continuously.

3. Turn down the heat to simmering and cook for 45 minutes. The chutney should be much thicker. If not, raise the heat so it is simmering more briskly and stir until it is thicker. This should take about 4–5 minutes.

4. Stir well and pot immediately in sterilised jars. Leave the chutney to mature for 2 weeks before eating.

Pickled Pears

This pickle is delicious served with cooked ham or cheese. It will keep unopened in the fridge for about four weeks, but once opened use within ten days.

Makes 2 x 450g jars

450g sugar
400ml white-wine
  vinegar
I teaspoon
  ground allspice
½ teaspoon cinnamon
Zest of I lemon,
  pared away from
  the pith in strips
  rather than grated
750g Conference or
  Comice pears,
  peeled and
  quartered

1. Put all the ingredients except the lemon zest and pears into a large pan and bring slowly to the boil, stirring all the time.

2. When the sugar has dissolved, add the pears and zest. Simmer for 10 minutes.

3. Spoon the pears into two sterilised screwtop jars and pour in the pickling liquid.

4. Seal the jars well, then label and date.

November can often seem a dark month. The summertime clocks have changed and the nights draw in. The very first toffee apples hit the market stalls and the serious treats of parkin and treacle toffee lead you in from Bonfire Night to the days of preparation for Christmas.

November delights in beans. The new season's crop is in the ground before we start to consume the current supply, and there are few better evening meals than a bowl of various pulses, flavoured with maybe a little ham, and some fine homemade bread, all of it washed down, perhaps, with the first pint of home-brewed ale, which was set brewing in August.

It is a terrible thing, thirst, yet this time of the year comes to the rescue. November is the first of the months that are 'planned for' in terms of bottle format, as 25 litres of sugar, water, hops and barley are fermented to yield a good, dark pint. The darkness comes from a kilo and a half of molasses, which, when fermented, produces a smoky nuttiness that leads one to wish the radiator was a real fire.

Sugar and dark fruit in November are also harbingers of one more tradition: Christmas cake. In countless homes across the country, a spare Saturday in the month will be given over to making the best cake of the year, fed lovingly every fortnight with brandy and hidden well away from greedy fingers.

November

November Menu

A three-course meal to serve 4 people

Clam and Crab Soup

Autumn Chicken

Apple and Prune Strudel

Clam and Crab Soup

If you have trouble getting hold of clams, use cockles out of the shells instead. They are already cooked, so can be added to the soup at the same time as the crabmeat.

300–350g clams
300ml fish stock
30g butter
1 onion, chopped
1 leek, thinly sliced
1 tablespoon
    plain flour
50ml dry white wine
300ml milk
Dash of Tabasco sauce
2 tablespoons freshly
    chopped parsley
200g crabmeat
4 tablespoons
    double cream

1. Put the clams in a lidded pan over a high heat and pour in some hot water to cover the bottom of the pan. Cover and cook for 4 minutes. Remove from the heat and check to see if all of them have opened; discard any that haven't. Cool and remove the meat from the shells. Pour the cooking liquor into the fish stock.

2. Melt the butter in a large pan and add the onions and leeks. Cook over a medium heat until tender.

3. Remove from the heat and sprinkle in the flour. Stir in well.

4. Return to a low heat and gradually add the stock, wine and milk. Bring to the boil and cook for 2 minutes.

5. Reduce the heat. Add the Tabasco sauce, cooked clams, parsley and crabmeat. Stir well and cook on a gentle heat for 3–4 minutes to allow the flavours to develop.

6. Serve with a swirl of cream and a few sprigs of parsley to garnish.

Autumn Chicken

A delicious and autumn-coloured dish. The apples, sage and onion go really well with the chicken, and the whole dish is wonderful served with sweetcorn and runner beans.

25g butter
1 tablespoon
  sunflower oil
1 onion, chopped
2 garlic cloves,
  chopped
350g long-grain rice
1 rounded teaspoon
  turmeric
3 chopped fresh
  sage leaves
  (or ½ teaspoon dried)
4 chicken breasts
2 tablespoons honey
1 Bramley apple or
  2 Worcesters,
  peeled, sliced and
  put into cold water
  with a squeeze of
  lemon juice
200ml dry cider
300ml hot
  chicken stock
Salt and pepper
  to taste

1. Preheat the oven to 180°C/gas mark 4.

2. Melt the butter with the oil in a large frying pan. Fry the onion and garlic gently for 2–3 minutes, or until the onion is soft.

3. Add the rice and sprinkle in the turmeric. Stir to coat the rice well in the turmeric and butter.

4. Stir in the sage and season with some salt and pepper. Pour the ingredients into a large ovenproof dish.

5. If the pan looks dry, add a little more oil and fry the chicken. Drizzle the honey evenly over it.

6. Add the apple slices. When the chicken has seared on both sides, pour in the cider and simmer for 3–4 minutes.

7. Put the chicken and apples on top of the rice and pour over the cider 'sauce'.

8. Stir in the stock and cover the dish with foil.

9. Cook for 35–40 minutes. Remove the foil and cook for 5 minutes longer.

Apple and Prune Strudel

A classic autumnal dessert that is best served with cream.

50g breadcrumbs
3 large dessert apples,
   peeled and chopped
2 tablespoons
   apple juice
100g pitted prunes,
   roughly chopped
50g raisins
4 tablespoons honey
2 tablespoons
   Armagnac
1 level teaspoon
   cinnamon
5 sheets filo pastry
30g butter

1. Preheat the oven to 190°C/gas mark 5. Lightly oil a baking sheet.

2. In a bowl, combine all the ingredients except for the pastry and butter. The mixture should be moist but not runny.

3. Melt the butter in a small pan.

4. Put 1 sheet of pastry on a clean surface and brush it with the butter. Lay another sheet fully over the top of this one to make a strong base and brush it with butter. Lay the next sheet offset to the right by about 3cm; brush with butter. Lay the next sheet again offset by 3cm; brush with butter. Finally, lay the last sheet over the top of the previous one with no offset and brush well with butter.

5. Spread the filling over the surface of the pastry, leaving about 2cm around the edge for overspill.

6. Roll up the strudel to form a sausage shape and dampen and seal the edges.

7. Put the strudel carefully on the baking sheet and bake for about 30 minutes until golden brown.

8. Cool for at least 15 minutes before serving.

Onion Soup

A creamy soup that really satisfies on a cold day. Serve this with a hunk of your favourite cheese and some crusty bread or slices of thin toast.

Serves 4–6

30g butter
600g onions,
   finely chopped
Salt and pepper
   to taste
1 litre chicken or
   vegetable stock
100ml single cream

1. Heat the butter in a saucepan and fry the onions until soft but not brown.

2. Season to taste with salt and pepper and stir in the stock.

3. Bring to the boil, stirring continuously, then simmer for 30 minutes.

4. Stir in the cream and serve.

Variation
For a slightly thicker soup, after softening the onions sprinkle 1 tablespoon of plain flour over them and stir well. Add the stock immediately, stirring continuously.

Sweetcorn Fritters

These are ideal to serve with fried chicken or bacon and eggs. They are equally tasty on their own as a snack. If you like them bubbly and risen, add half a teaspoon of baking powder to the batter before stirring in the corn.

Make 4 fritters

2 large ears of corn
60g plain flour
Pinch of salt
Pinch of black pepper
   or cayenne pepper
l egg
50ml milk
2 tablespoons
   single cream
2–3 tablespoons
   sunflower oil

1. Boil the corn in water for about 8 minutes. Remove from the water and allow to cool until handleable.

2. Stand the corn over a bowl or on a chopping board and use a sharp knife to cut the kernels away from the cob. Put to one side.

3. Sift the flour, salt and pepper into a bowl.

4. Whisk the egg, milk and cream together until bubbly.

5. Beat this into the flour mixture until it is smooth. Stir in the corn.

6. Heat the oil in a large frying pan and ladle or spoon the mixture into the pan. Make 4 equal-sized fritters and fry on each side for about 2 minutes, or until golden brown.

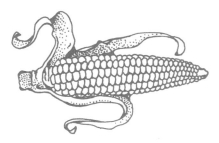

Crab and Prawn Quiche

This makes a delicious lunch or buffet dish served with coleslaw (see page 36).

Serves 4

200g shortcrust pastry
15g butter
1 small leek,
    finely chopped
3 eggs
100ml double cream
A pinch of cayenne
    pepper (more if you
    like a bigger kick)
1 tablespoon
    chives, chopped
180g crabmeat
12 large prawns
Salt and black
    pepper to taste

1. Preheat the oven to 190°C/gas mark 5. Grease a 20cm quiche tin.

2. Roll out the pastry and bake it blind (see page 156) for 15 minutes.

3. Heat the butter in a saucepan or frying pan and fry the leeks over a medium heat until soft. Spread onto the base of the pastry case.

4. Beat the eggs, cream and cayenne pepper together. Stir in the chives.

5. Arrange the crabmeat over the leeks. Pour the cream mixture on top.

6. Add the prawns in among the crab. Put on a baking sheet.

7. Bake in the oven for 30–35 minutes, or until the filling is set. Cool for 20 minutes before serving hot, or serve cold.

Squash and Celeriac Lasagne

A vegetarian lasagne that makes the most of rich autumn vegetables such as butternut squash.

Serves 4

400g celeriac, cut into
   small chunks
I small butternut
   squash, peeled
   and cubed
3 tablespoons olive oil
10g butter
I onion
2 garlic cloves
300ml passata
200ml vegetable stock
I teaspoon oregano
   or marjoram
Salt and pepper to taste
12 sheets of lasagne

For the white sauce
20g butter
I tablespoon
   plain flour
½ teaspoon dry
   mustard powder
   or I teaspoon
   English mustard
450ml milk
100g Cheddar, grated
50g fresh
   Parmesan, grated
Salt and pepper
   to taste

1. Preheat the oven to 190°C/gas mark 5.

2. Put the celeriac and squash in a roasting pan and coat in the olive oil. Roast for about 25 minutes, or until the vegetables are just tender.

3. Meanwhile, melt the butter in a pan and fry the onion and garlic together gently over a low–medium heat.

4. Add the cooked celeriac and squash to the onions and stir well.

5. Add the passata, stock and herbs. Season with salt and pepper and simmer everything together for 10 minutes.

To make the sauce
1. Melt the butter in a pan over a low heat and stir in the flour and mustard.

2. Gradually add the milk and stir well. Raise the heat and bring to the boil, stirring continuously.

3. Add half the cheese, check the seasoning and adjust if necessary.

To assemble the lasagne
1. Spoon half the vegetable mixture into a lasagne tin or dish.

2. Put 4 sheets of lasagne on top and repeat this with another layer of vegetables, followed by one of lasagne. Pour the white sauce over the top and sprinkle with the rest of the cheese.

3. Bake for about 40 minutes, or until the top is brown and bubbling and the pasta is tender.

Yorkshire Parkin

Autumn wouldn't be the same without some sticky parkin, especially on Bonfire Night! Parkin develops a stickiness if left for 24 hours before eating, and the flavour is better for it. So try to make this the day before you want to eat it.

Makes 12 squares

1 level teaspoon
   ground ginger
130g self-raising flour
50g butter
2 tablespoons
   black treacle
2 tablespoons
   golden syrup
50g brown sugar
130g fine oatmeal
1 egg
2 tablespoons milk

1. Grease a 15cm square tin. Preheat the oven to 170°C/gas mark 3.

2. Sieve the ginger with the flour into a large mixing bowl.

3. Melt the butter with the treacle, syrup and sugar in a pan over a very low heat. As soon as the butter has melted, remove from the heat, stir well and beat in the egg.

4. Pour the buttery mixture into the flour and mix vigorously with a wooden spoon.

5. Add the milk and beat again; it should be a soft, easily poured mixture. If not, add another tablespoon of milk.

6. Pour the mixture into the tin and bake for 50–55 minutes; it should be firm to the touch in the centre when cooked. If not, bake for 5 more minutes.

7. Cool in the tin on a cooling rack. After 10 minutes, cut the cake into 12 equal squares.

8. When completely cool, lift the squares out of the tin and transfer to an airtight storage tin.

Spiced Pumpkin Cake

This is a moist, creamy-tasting cake. This recipe uses a mascarpone cheese filling, but it can be made without one because it is so flavoursome. The cake will need to be stored in the fridge and may be kept for up to three days.

Makes 8–10 portions

500g fresh pumpkin,
   peeled and cut
   into chunks
300g self-raising flour
1 level teaspoon
   cinnamon
1 level teaspoon
   mixed spice
50g raisins
25g currants
50g walnuts
150g butter
250g soft brown sugar
3 eggs
4 tablespoons milk

For the filling
1 teaspoon
   vanilla extract
150g mascarpone
   cheese
50g icing sugar

1. Preheat the oven to 180°C/gas mark 4. Grease and line 2 x 20cm sandwich tins.

2. Bake the pumpkin in the oven on a baking sheet for about 40 minutes until tender. Cool, then purée until smooth. If the purée is very watery, simmer in a pan to evaporate some of the liquid for about 10 minutes, then leave to cool completely.

3. Sift the flour and spices together into a large mixing bowl.

4. Combine the fruit and nuts together in a separate bowl and stir in 1 dessertspoon of the flour.

5. Cream the butter and sugar together until light and fluffy. Sprinkle in 1 tablespoon of flour, then beat in the eggs gradually.

6. Fold in half of the flour then the pumpkin purée, then the rest of the flour.

7. Stir in the fruit and nut mixture and add enough of the milk to give the cake a 'dropping consistency' – it should drop off the spoon easily.

8. Divide the mixture equally between the tins, and bake for 25–30 minutes, or until risen and springy to the touch.

9. When cooked, leave to cool in the tins for 15 minutes, then transfer to a cooling rack.

For the filling
1. Beat the vanilla extract into the cheese for a few seconds to loosen the texture. Sift in the icing sugar and beat into the cheese until smooth.

2. When the cakes are cold, use the filling to sandwich them together.

Variation
If you want to make a large cake, grease and line a deeper 2cm round loose-bottomed tin. Spoon all the mixture into the tin and bake for 50 minutes to 1 hour. Again, the cake should be springy to the touch in the centre when it is cooked.

Treacle Toffee

This is another Bonfire Night necessity. Just make sure everyone cleans their teeth before going to bed! This can be made a few days before serving if required.

Makes about 28 pieces

500g golden caster
   sugar or soft
   brown sugar
4 tablespoons
   dark treacle
125g unsalted butter
1 x 372g tin
   condensed milk
3 dessertspoons water

1. Butter an 18cm x 26cm rectangular tin and line it with baking paper.

2. Put all the ingredients into a large, heavy-based pan over a low heat. Stir gently until all the sugar has dissolved. Check the back of the spoon for sugar crystals; once there are no crystals showing, the mixture is ready to bring to the boil.

3. Turn up the heat and continue to cook. When the mixture reaches a rolling boil, continue boiling for 4 minutes, either with a preserving thermometer or in the following way: have a bowl of iced water ready and, after 3–4 minutes of boiling, drop a little of the mixture into the water; when it forms a firm ball, the toffee is ready. If you have a thermometer, it needs to reach 130°C or a firm-ball consistency. This will good and chewy, but won't break your teeth!

4. When the right stage has been reached, remove from the heat and allow the bubbling to subside before pouring the toffee into the tin.

5. When cool, leave in the tin and cut the toffee into bite-sized squares (a strong fish slice lifts it easily). This may need to be repeated as the cuts tend to disappear as it cools. Once completely cold, break up the pieces and wrap each in greaseproof paper. Store in an airtight tin until ready to serve.

Cranberry Jelly

Ideal for making in preparation for Christmas. It goes so well with roast poultry and ham.

Makes 4–5 x 450g jars

1.5kg cranberries
500ml water
Sugar: 80g per
100ml of juice

1. Cook the cranberries and water at simmering for about 2 minutes, or until the fruit is soft.

2. Strain the juice for 3–4 hours, or until the juice stops dripping through the strainer. Measure the juice, then weigh out the correct amount of sugar.

3. Put the juice in the pan with the sugar over a gentle heat and stir until all the sugar has dissolved.

5. Turn up the heat and boil rapidly for 10 minutes. Check for setting point (see page 19).

6. Cool for about 5 minutes before bottling in sterilised jars. Label and date.

Easy Christmas Cake

This is the most foolproof Christmas cake you could make, so don't be afraid just have a go at it. It does need to be made about 6 weeks in advance of Christmas – which means early November is the ideal time to make it.

**Makes about
20 portions**

225g butter
225g soft brown sugar
1 tablespoon
  black treacle
265g plain white flour
  plus 2 rounded
  teaspoons baking
  powder, sieved
  together in a bowl
5 eggs, well beaten
Zest and juice of
  1 lemon
1 level teaspoon
  cinnamon
½ teaspoon mixed spice
½ teaspoon freshly
  grated nutmeg
1kg dried fruit of your
  choice; raisins,
  currants, sultanas,
  glacé cherries,
  cranberries,
  pineapples, etc.
50g ground almonds
50g chopped almonds
Brandy, for feeding
  the cake

1. Preheat oven to 160°C/gas 3 and prepare your cake tin as follows: lightly grease a 24cm round or 20cm square tin. Springform tins are easiest to use for this purpose, but any type will do. Line the tin with 1 layer of baking paper and wrap aluminium foil around the outside, squeezing it to fit closely. Tie a double layer of brown or greaseproof paper around the outside over the foil and above the tin lip to extend about 5cm.

2. Cream the butter, sugar and treacle together in a large mixing bowl.

3. Stir in 4 tablespoons of the flour and beat in the eggs, lemon zest and juice.

4. Add the spices to the rest of the flour and stir well.

5. Add the fruit and nuts to the flour to coat and stir into the creamed mixture. Make sure all are well distributed through the mixture.

6. Spoon the cake mixture into the tin, carefully pressing it down gently and smoothing over the top. Make a small depression in the centre. This gives a level top to the finished cake.

7. Put the tin on a baking sheet and place it in the centre of the oven. Turn the heat down to 150°C/gas mark 2 and bake for 30 minutes.

8. Turn the heat down again to 140°C/gas mark 1 and bake for 2 hours. Test to see if it is cooked by pushing a metal skewer through the centre. If the cake is done, the skewer will come out clean with no cake mixture attached. If bits of mixture are clinging to it, then bake for a further 30 minutes and test again. Repeat as necessary until the cake is completely baked through.

9. Put the cake on a cooling rack and leave in the tin to cool for about 2 hours.

10. Remove the cake from the tin and leave it to cool completely before removing all the paper.

11. Stand for 30 minutes before pricking the cake all over with a metal skewer and pouring tablespoons of brandy down the holes. Wrap in a layer of greaseproof paper and a layer of foil and store in an airtight tin.

12. Repeat the process of 'feeding' the cake with brandy twice more, each time leaving the cake to stand for two weeks before repeating and wrapping the cake securely again.

Apple Roly Poly

Serve this dessert hot with custard for a real autumn pick-me-up.

Serves 6

For the pastry
200g self-raising flour
A pinch salt
100g vegetarian suet
Water to mix to a
   soft dough

For the fruit filling
2 medium Bramley
   apples, peeled,
   cored and diced
100ml apple juice
50g golden
   caster sugar

1. First, make the pastry by sieving the flour and salt together into a bowl. Stir in the suet.

2. Add 2 tablespoons of water and stir in. Continue adding a little water to make a soft dough that you will be able to roll out lightly.

3. Use your hands to gather the mixture into a ball, then knead very lightly until smooth.

4. Preheat the oven to 200°C/gas mark 6.

5. Mix the filling ingredients together and spread the mixture over the surface of the pastry, leaving the edges clear or it will ooze out. Dampen the edges and roll up.

6. Place on a greased baking sheet and bake for 30–40 minutes.

Quince Jam

Quinces are very hard fruits; they look like wrinkly pears and are not good to eat raw. Yet when cooked, they make excellent jellies and jams. They have a honey flavour but aren't sweet so require plenty of sugar. The pectin content is high in quinces, so they don't need any extra added to the jam. They are also good for combining with fruit that has a low pectin content, such as pears, to make jam.

Makes 6 x 450g jars

2kg quinces, peeled, cored and diced
1.5 litres water
Juice of 2 lemons
3kg sugar

1. Put the fruit and water in a large preserving pan and bring to the boil. Turn down the heat and simmer for 1–1¼ hours. Cover to stop the water from evaporating too quickly.

2. When the fruit is tender, stir in the sugar and lemon juice. Add the sugar gradually, stirring constantly, until it has all dissolved.

3. Continue to simmer until the mixture begins to thicken, then bring to the boil.

4. Boil for 5 minutes, remove from the heat, then test for setting point (see page 19). Boil again if it isn't ready – this time for 2 minutes – remove from the heat and test again. Repeat this until it reaches setting point.

5. Cool for 10 minutes, then stir and pot into sterilised jars. Label and date. This should keep for at least a year unopened, but once opened, store in the fridge and use within 4 weeks.

December brings with it the first frosts of the season, and most plants go into an irrevocable decline, save for beans and onions, which simply stop growing and sit it out, and garlic, which revels in the cold and never felt better. The colder you can get garlic, the better: you get better flavour and consistency of bulbs.

December is muddy-boot month; there is so much to do with your feet. Sprouts in danger of exploding in the winter sun are gathered into tight buttons by firming them into the soil with the heel so that they do not rock about. Winter cabbages need the same treatment. The temptation to walk over the soil must be kept to a minimum, however, if disease isn't to be trampled all over the plot.

Cold water brings split, hard knuckles and wonderful sea fish. We are blessed with the very best seafood in the UK. Everyone in the world eats our fish, from Devonian pilchards to Lancastrian cockles. Our West Country eels, and their young elvers, are prized so much that they are worth their weight in gold, and our young lobster and scallops from Scotland are simply the best. If only Christmas dinner could be a seafood dish!

The truth is, you cannot beat our produce, which, when taken seasonally, is the best anywhere. So move over, all you complex cuisines who think you're something special. The best seasonal food in the world comes from the most beautiful country in the world: good old Blighty.

December

December Menu

A Christmas Dinner to serve 6 people

Port-soaked Melon

Roast Turkey with all the Trimmings

Christmas Pudding with Brandy Sauce

Port-soaked Melon

A wonderful start to a celebration meal. If you wish to serve this to children and would prefer not to use port, make it with their favourite fresh fruit juice instead.

Serves 6–8

2 small melons:
  honeydew,
  cantaloupe,
  Charentais or ogen
2 dessertspoons
  soft brown sugar
  (or less if you wish)
150ml port

1. Cut the melons in thirds or quarters and scoop out the seeds.

2. Place each piece either in a large bowl or separate bowls and score the flesh with a sharp knife one way and crisscross the other way. This makes eating the melon easier and allows the port to seep into the flesh quicker.

3. Sprinkle the sugar evenly over the top of the melons.

4. Drizzle the port generously over the melon. Chill in the fridge for at least an hour before serving.

Roast Turkey with all the Trimmings

This recipe cooks the bird without any dryness, as the water steams it from beneath while it roasts. Stuffing a turkey can often make it take too long to cook, so in this recipe, cook your stuffing separately and serve it as an accompaniment.

I x 4–4.5kg turkey
250g butter
8 rashers streaky bacon
2 lemons
I litre hot water

To make the gravy
4 level teaspoons of
   flour or gravy
   powder per
   300ml stock

1. Preheat the oven to 180°C/gas mark 4.

2. Place the turkey in a large roasting pan and slip your hand under the skin of the breast to make a gap right down to the legs. Push half the butter under each side of the breast skin down to the leg meat and spread the butter out so that some covers the leg and the breast meat.

3. Lay 3 rashers of the bacon over each breast and 1 around the leg. Cut the lemons in half and place them inside the cavity of the bird.

4. Pour the hot water into the roasting pan around the bird. Cover the turkey with foil and put in the oven. Cooking times are 20 minutes per 450g, plus an extra 20 minutes. (A stuffed bird should take between 30–50 minutes longer.)

5. Push a skewer into the thickest part of the thigh joint; the juices should run clear if it's done. If there is any trace of redness, it needs a little longer in the oven, but be sure to check it again after 15 minutes.

6. When cooked, leave to rest for at least 30 minutes before carving. Serve with roasted potatoes and fresh vegetables prepared and cooked to your taste.

To make the gravy
1. Mix the flour or gravy powder with a little cold water to make a thin paste.

2. Bring the stock you are using to the boil, turn down the heat and stir in the paste. Add a little red wine, port or brandy for extra flavour if you wish and check the seasoning; adjust if necessary.

3. Simmer for 4 minutes, then serve immediately.

The Trimmings

No Christmas dinner is complete without the trimmings, so here are four recipes to provide the finishing touches to your meal.

All the trimmings recipes serve 6

12 thin pork sausages
12 rashers
  streaky bacon

Sausage and Bacon Rolls

Make these at the last minute and cook them with the roast potatoes. Also make sure that there are at least two for each person.

1. Preheat the oven to 200°C/gas mark 6.

2. Wrap each sausage in a rasher of bacon and place on a rack over a roasting pan. Cook for about 25 minutes, or until the bacon is crispy.

280ml milk
Half a very small
  onion, finely chopped
1 bay leaf
4 cloves
Salt and pepper
  to taste
60g white
  breadcrumbs
50g butter
1 tablespoon
  single cream
A little grated nutmeg
  for serving

Bread Sauce

Use more or less of the breadcrumb amount, depending on how thick you like your sauce.

1. Put the milk in a small pan with the onions, bay leaf, cloves and seasoning and bring to just boiling; then turn down the heat and simmer for 5 minutes.

2. Turn off the heat, pour into a bowl and leave for 30 minutes to allow all the flavours to infuse.

3. Put the breadcrumbs in an ovenproof serving dish.

4. Strain the milk back into the pan and add the butter. Heat until the butter melts and the milk is hot. Stir in the cream and pour it over the breadcrumbs.

5. Finish with a little grated nutmeg.

300g chestnuts
2 chicken livers
50g breadcrumbs
100g butter

Chestnut Stuffing

1. Slit the chestnuts around the side to aid cooking. Put them in a pan with just enough water to cover and simmer until they are tender. This will take about 30 minutes. Cool until they are handleable and remove the shells.

2. Pound the chestnuts with a pestle and mortar, or put them in a blender and grind them to a coarse texture. Transfer to a bowl, and preheat the oven to 180°C/gas mark 4.

3. Chop the chicken livers finely and add to the chestnuts. Stir in the breadcrumbs, melt the butter and pour over the stuffing mixture and combine with a spoon. Press down into an ovenproof dish and bake for 20 minutes.

30g butter
2 small onions,
   finely chopped
100g fresh
   breadcrumbs
2 tablespoons fresh
   sage leaves,
   finely chopped
Salt and pepper
   to taste

Sage and Onion Stuffing

The freshness of the sage makes all the difference to the taste here. Add a couple of tablespoons of turkey juices to the stuffing for even more flavour.

1. Heat the butter in a pan and fry the onions until very soft but not brown. Remove from the heat.

2. Add the breadcrumbs and sage and stir well. Add any juices from the turkey at this point if you wish. Season to taste.

3. Place in an ovenproof dish and heat about 10 minutes prior to serving at 180°C/gas mark 4.

Christmas Pudding

Making your own pudding for Christmas is very satisfying. This recipe needs to be made about three weeks in advance. Because there are so many ingredients, it helps to list them in the order they're added. Also weigh and prepare all ingredients beforehand, and arrange them in the order they're added to the mixture – then, hopefully, nothing will be forgotten! Mix the pudding in the evening before cooking the following morning, as it needs to steam for about seven hours.

Serves 6–8

50g self-raising flour
½ level teaspoon
   mixed spice
½ level teaspoon
   cinnamon
¼ teaspoon
   grated nutmeg
110g vegetarian suet
180g soft brown sugar
110g freshly made
   brown breadcrumbs
110g each raisins,
   sultanas and currants
25g glacé cherries,
   halved or whole
25g candied peel
50g chopped almonds
Zest and juice of
   1 lemon and 1 orange
1 cooking apple, peeled,
   cored and diced
1 medium carrot, grated
2 large eggs
1 tablespoon
   black treacle
150ml dark ale
3 tablespoons brandy
   or rum

1. Sift the flour and spices together in a large mixing bowl. Stir in the suet, sugar and breadcrumbs.

2. Mix the dried and candied fruit and nuts together in a separate bowl, then stir into the dry ingredients. Add the lemon and orange juice and zest and stir well. Mix in the apple and carrot.

3. Beat the eggs in a jug or bowl and stir in the treacle, ale and brandy. Add the egg mixture to the other ingredients and stir well for a few minutes until everything is well-combined. Cover the bowl and leave overnight to infuse.

4. Grease a 1.2-litre pudding bowl and pack the mixture into it well, pressing it down. Place a disc of baking parchment on top to fit slightly up the sides of the basin. Use a double layer of greaseproof paper over the top of the basin and tie securely with string. Finish with a layer of foil and also tie this with string.

5. Place the pudding in a steamer over boiling water. Reduce the heat to simmering and cover with the lid. Steam for 7 hours. Top up the water levels in the pan with boiling water as needed.

6. Remove from the steamer and leave to cool for 1 hour, then remove the wrappings and leave to cool completely.

7. When cool, wrap in 2 layers of greaseproof paper and store in a cool, dark place for at least 3 weeks before eating.

8. To reheat, put in a steamer and cook for 2–2½ hours or heat in a microwave for 5–6 minutes until piping hot. Serve with brandy sauce.

Brandy Sauce

Using evaporated milk instead of ordinary milk gives the sauce a much creamier flavour.

Serves 6–8

400ml evaporated milk, made up to 650ml with water
2 tablespoons brown sugar
2 tablespoons cornflour mixed with 4 tablespoons of the milk mixture: (2 rounded tablespoons for a reasonably thick sauce, 2 level tablespoons for a thinner one)
4–6 tablespoons brandy or rum

1. Heat the milk in a saucepan until almost boiling. Remove from the heat, then whisk the sugar and cornflour mixture into the hot milk.

2. Bring the sauce to boiling point, stirring continuously, then simmer for 2 minutes.

3. Remove from the heat and stir in the brandy or rum. Serve with Christmas pudding.

Lentil and Bacon Soup

Dried vegetables and pulses come into their own during the months when fresh vegetables are at their less abundant. Always having lentils, peas and various kinds of beans on hand means you can make a hearty soup or casserole any time.

Serves 4

4 rashers back bacon
2 rashers
    streaky bacon
A little oil for frying
I medium onion,
    finely chopped
I garlic clove, chopped
2 celery sticks,
    chopped
2 carrots, chopped
I dessertspoon
    tomato purée
1.5 litres vegetable
    stock
5 tablespoons lentils
Salt and pepper
    to taste

1. Fry the bacon in the oil until cooked. Add the onion, garlic, celery and carrot. Cook on a low heat for 10 minutes.

2. Stir in the tomato purée.

3. Gradually stir in the stock, then stir in the lentils.

4. Bring to the boil, stirring continuously as the lentils can rest on the bottom of the pan and stick. Turn down the heat to simmering and cook for 40 minutes, stirring occasionally.

5. Check the seasoning and adjust it if necessary. Black pepper really enhances the flavour of this soup. Serve immediately or store in the fridge for 2–3 days.

Butter Bean Pâté

This is a quick and easy pâté for lunch or as a starter. It is particularly good for vegetarians.

Serves 4

400g dried butter
  beans, soaked for
  4 hours, then
  simmered until
  tender – about
  I hour – and
  cooled completely
Juice of half a lemon
I garlic clove, grated
I rounded teaspoon
  fresh mint, chopped
I tablespoon olive oil
Salt and black pepper
  to taste

1. Put the beans and lemon juice in a food processor and blend for about 10 seconds, then add the other ingredients and continue to blend until a smooth paste is formed. You can do this with a masher and fork, but it won't be as smooth.

2. Put the pâté into small ramekins and serve with bread or melba toast.

Pork with Beans

This is good served with baked potatoes or boiled rice.

Serves 6

450g dried haricot
  beans, soaked in
  plenty of cold
  water overnight
2 tablespoons
  sunflower oil
I onion, finely chopped
500g pork steak, cut
  into cubes
2 rashers of streaky
  bacon, chopped
500ml beef or
  vegetable stock
I garlic clove, chopped
½ level teaspoon
  dried oregano
½ level teaspoon
  dried thyme
I level dessertspoon
  brown sugar
I x 400g can
  plum tomatoes
Salt and pepper
  to taste

1. Preheat the oven 160°C/gas mark 2.

2. Drain the beans of their steeping water and boil in fresh water for 10 minutes.

3. Heat the oil in a pan and fry the onion, pork and bacon until the pork has changed colour. Place in a lidded casserole.

4. Drain the beans and stir them into the pork mixture.

5. Heat the stock in the frying pan and add the garlic, herbs, sugar and can of tomatoes. Chop the tomatoes into small pieces as they heat in the stock, or do this separately before adding to the pan. Bring everything to the boil, then pour it over the meat and bean mixture. Season to taste.

6. Cover and cook for 3 hours. Stir, then cook for another 40–50 minutes.

Winter Fish Pie

A fish pie made with very thin puff pastry.

Serves 4–6

450g white fish:
    haddock, pollack,
    cod or coley, or a
    combination
100ml milk
Pinch of salt
120g cockles
120g mussels
300g puff pastry
50g spinach
3 eggs
80ml single cream
1 tablespoon parsley
Salt and black pepper
    to taste
50g Cheddar, grated

1. Preheat the oven to 200°C/gas mark 6. Grease a deep pie dish.

2. Poach the fish in the milk with a pinch of salt for 5–6 minutes, until it begins to flake. Lift the fish out of the milk and place in a bowl to cool slightly. Reserve the poaching liquid.

3. Combine the cockles and mussels and add them to the cooked fish.

4. Roll out two-thirds of the pastry as thinly as is handleable and line the pie dish with it, carefully pushing the pastry down to get rid of any air bubbles. Pile the fish mixture into the pie dish on top of the pastry.

5. Scatter the spinach over the fish evenly and press down gently.

6. Beat the eggs and cream together and stir in the poaching liquid.

7. Season with pepper and check for salt: remember that the cheese will be salty.

8. Pour the egg mixture over the fish and sprinkle the cheese over everything. Stir gently to combine.

9. Roll out the pastry lid. Moisten the edges of the pie, top with the lid and seal the edges. Bake for 30–40 minutes until well-risen and golden brown.

10. Serve immediately with a watercress salad drizzled with a tablespoon of balsamic vinegar or lemon juice.

Vegetable and Green Lentil Curry

This makes a filling meal when served with boiled rice, naan bread or some chapatis.

Serves 4–5

50g butter
1 large onion, chopped
3 garlic cloves, chopped
½ teaspoon chilli flakes
1 teaspoon
   ground cumin
1 teaspoon
   ground coriander
3 green cardamom pods
1 tablespoon turmeric
1 teaspoon
   garam masala
2 tablespoons
   tomato purée
2 carrots, chopped
2 medium
   potatoes, diced
1 small swede, peeled
   and chopped
8 Brussels sprouts,
   chopped
Salt and pepper
   to taste
1 x 400g can chopped
   plum tomatoes
400ml vegetable stock
150g green lentils
100g mushrooms,
   halved

1. Melt the butter in a large pan over a low heat and add the onion, garlic and all the spices. Stir in the tomato purée and cook for a few minutes.

2. Add the carrots, potatoes, swede and Brussels sprouts and season with salt and pepper. Cook for 10 minutes, allowing the vegetables to sweat.

3. Raise the temperature to a medium heat and stir in the tomatoes and stock.

4. Bring to the boil, then stir in the lentils. Turn down the heat, cover and simmer for 30 minutes.

5. Add the mushrooms and simmer for 15 more minutes.

6. Allow to settle for 5 minutes before serving.

Babas with Orange and Rum Syrup

These are a wonderful winter pudding and can be served instead of or alongside Christmas pudding.

Serves 6

120g plain white flour
Half a sachet
   (3.5g) fast-acting
   dried yeast
25g soft brown sugar
15g butter, melted
80ml warm milk
2 eggs, beaten
Zest and juice of
   1 orange

For the syrup
100ml fresh
   orange juice
60g golden
   caster sugar
2 tablespoons rum
Very thin strips of
   orange peel: zest
   only – no pith

1. Butter a 6-hole muffin tin.

2. Sift the flour into a bowl and stir in the yeast and sugar,

3. Combine the melted butter and warm milk and beat in the eggs, orange zest and juice. Pour the liquid into the flour mixture and beat in well.

4. Pour the baba mixture into the muffin cases and leave in a warm place to rise.

5. Preheat the oven to 200°C/gas mark 6.

6. When the babas have risen nearly to the top of the tins, bake for about 15 minutes.

7. Make the syrup by putting the orange juice, sugar and thin strips of orange peel in a pan. Heat gently, stirring, until the sugar has dissolved.

8. Bring to the boil for 2 minutes, then remove from the heat and stir in the rum.

9. When the babas are cooked, remove from the tin carefully and put them in a serving dish or dishes. Prick them all over the surface while still hot and drizzle the sauce over them evenly.

10. Leave for 10 minutes to allow the sauce to infuse before serving warm with cream.

Apples and Pears Pudding

This is wonderful served hot with cream or custard.

Serves 4

450g mixture of apples and pears, peeled and diced
2 tablespoons honey or soft brown sugar
80g butter, at room temperature
80g golden caster sugar
120g self-raising flour
1 egg, beaten
3 tablespoons milk

1. Preheat the oven to 180°C/gas mark 4.

2. Put the fruit in a pan with the sugar or honey and heat gently until the sugar has dissolved, if that's what you are using. Otherwise, bring the fruit to the boil and then simmer for 5 minutes.

3. Cool. Butter a 1.2 litre pudding basin and spoon the fruit into the bottom.

4. Cream the butter and caster sugar together until light and fluffy. Sift a tablespoon of the flour into the creamed mixture and beat in the egg.

5. Add the rest of the flour and fold in with a metal spoon.

6. Stir in the milk and spread the mixture over the prepared fruit.

7. Bake for 45 minutes, or until the top of the sponge is springy to the touch.

Mulled Ale

This is more like a meal than a drink. It was traditionally given to travellers who needed reviving after journeying through terrible winter weather. Innkeepers often served this for free, hoping customers would spend more of their money once revived.

Serves 2

2 eggs
600ml brown ale
A little grated nutmeg
A knob of
    butter, optional
2 teaspoons
    caster sugar

1. Beat the eggs and add 3 tablespoons of the ale.

2. Heat the rest of the ale in a pan and stir in the nutmeg and butter, if using. Do not boil; just reach a hot but drinkable temperature.

3. Whisk the hot ale into the egg mixture, stir and serve immediately in mugs, with a teaspoon of caster sugar in each.

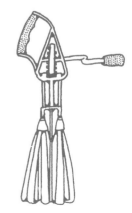

Spicy Winter Punch

Another winter warmer, but this time without any alcohol added – although you can certainly include some if you wish!

Makes 8–10 servings

3 apples, peeled and
  sliced very thinly
3 pears, peeled and
  sliced thinly
4 tangerines or
  satsumas, segmented,
  pith removed
100g green grapes,
  halved
30g golden
  caster sugar
1 litre apple juice
1 litre ginger ale
½ teaspoon cinnamon
A pinch grated nutmeg

1. Put all the ingredients in a large pan and heat to a gentle simmer.

2. Simmer for 2 minutes, then serve at once while still warm. Add a couple of tablespoons of rum or brandy if you like.

Tangerine Marmalade

This is a change from orange marmalade and can be prepared with any of the winter citrus fruits. Adding pectin is necessary, as some small citrus fruits lack it and the marmalade wouldn't set properly without it. This should keep for about a year unopened. Once opened, store in the fridge and keep for up to six weeks.

Makes 5 x 450g jars

1.5kg tangerines
4 lemons
2.8 litres water
1.5kg sugar
7g dried pectin
   (or half a sachet)

1. Cut all the fruit in half and squeeze out the juice. Put any pips in a muslin bag and tie securely. Leave the lemons in half, but slice the tangerines as thinly as possible, especially the peel.

2. Put the fruit, peel and pip bag in a large saucepan. Add the water and allow to steep for 4 hours.

3. Bring to the boil, then simmer for 1½ hours, or until the peel is tender.

4. Remove the lemon peel and muslin bag with tongs. Squeeze out all the juice, which will be slimy, and return it to the pan.

5. Stir in the sugar and pectin and put on to a low heat. Stir until the sugar dissolves.

6. Bring to the boil, then boil for 10 minutes. Test for setting point (see page 19).

7. Ladle into sterilised jars, then label and date.

The best motivation for starting a vegetable plot is the fantastic variety of foods you can grow. One of the most appropriate starting points when growing for the first time is to base your vegetable choice around what you like to eat. Sunday lunch, whether it's a salad, a curry or a full-blown British roast, is the ideal way to sort your plan.

It's hard to beat the pleasure derived from fresh vegetables you have grown yourself. Watching your crops develop from seedlings adds a seasoning to your food that no one else could ever truly understand – unless they, too, tried to grow their own.

Fresh Garden Produce

Growing Vegetables

How much space?

You'll find that growing a lot of your vegetables requires quite a modest space. There's no minimum size for a veg garden, but a 10m² plot will give you quite a lot of produce. Of course, if you can double this, so much the better. As a rough guide, plan on a third of your plot containing potatoes of various kinds, then divide the rest into ten sections grouped together, with cabbages and cauliflowers in one group; turnips, swedes, parsnips and carrots in another; peas, beans and salads in another; and, finally, onions and shallots bringing up the rear.

When to start?

Right now, regardless of the time of the year! Start slowly while you steadily plan and prepare the plot for greater things next year.

If your plot is overgrown, clear away a tenth of it and plant some salad items, such as lettuce and radishes, and pop in some garlic cloves all around the edge to deter slugs. If the plot isn't too bad, buy some cabbage plants from the garden centre and plant them at 60cm intervals with rows 60cm apart, and finely dig a patch of soil and sow some carrot seed.

Compost heap

There's a lot said about compost heaps. One of the easiest to make consists of three wooden pallets joined to make a U-shaped enclosure. Put a layer of newspaper at the bottom, then vegetable matter on the top. For every six inches of material, add another layer of newspaper, and soak it with a bucket of water. (If you can dare to add some urine to the water, so much the better!).

Other first planting ideas

Try sowing radish Mino Early, which is a winter radish and will do well if planted at any time of the year.

Lettuce and cabbage varieties called All the Year Round do well if planted at any time of the year. Don't worry too much about planting times; just pop them in the soil and see what you get; you should certainly have a decent first crop.

By August, clear a space for Japanese onions. These will be ready for lifting in the early summer, by which time you'll be ready for more traditional varieties such as Sturon.

Start to plan

Decide on where your potatoes are going to be planted next year, and mulch that area with rotted manure 20cm thick, then cover with some old carpet if you can to keep the weeds down.

Over the winter, clear your plot of weeds, make the soil good by adding compost and then mark out with sand the beds you're planning. If you can, spend the coming months talking to other vegetable gardeners, just to see how they do it.

Varietal suggestions

The following are all easy-grow varieties.

Beans Opera

Broccoli Boltardy

Carrots Nantes

Cabbage All the Year Round

Lettuce and other salads Try whatever takes your fancy on the shelf; they're all easy to grow.

Onions Sturon

Peas Kelvedon Wonder

Potatoes *Early* Rocket; *Maincrop* Maris Piper

Shallots Prisma

Swedes Magres

Turnips Imperial Green Globe, Snowball

Once you've chosen your varieties, you'll be ready to set about the business of growing and caring for your vegetables – which is why, on the following pages, you'll find a brief guide to doing just that.

BEANS

There are lots of different kinds of beans, each of which has a place in the garden and, thus, the kitchen. Broad beans are a favourite, as are runner beans and French dwarf types, which are an invention of the last century.

All beans are hungry plants and need plenty of rich, well-rotted manure. Traditionally, runner beans are sown into a trench, which for the previous six months housed rotting vegetable waste; by the time the seeds are sown, this 'waste' has become rich compost. The sow-in-a-cup method (see below) is, however, a lot easier.

Broad beans

Sow these in drinks cups or 8cm pots indoors in April. Use two seeds per pot and water them in. Discard the slower-growing plant in each pot. Prepare the bed where the plants will grow by incorporating plenty of compost. Plant out in May in a 'double row' – i.e. 40cm apart with the next row about 40cm away. The next double row starts 60cm further on.

Water when there is no rain. The plants flower after about 6 weeks and fruit will set a fortnight later. Guard against blackfly – the best way is to use netting. Collect the bean pods when they have obviously filled out.

You can also sow broad beans in September, directly in the ground, which has been prepared in the same way. The seedlings will grow to a couple of inches and then stop growing for a few months, but they are quite hardy and in the spring will shoot up to give an early crop at the end of May or early June.

Runner beans

Start off in pots just like broad beans. Prepare the ground in the same way, too. Provide a support of canes about 2m tall. This can take the form of a 'wigwam'. You need about 45cm between plants.

In May transplant the growing runner beans, one per cane. They grow up the canes and produce flowers and fruit. Once the beans are long enough, pick them. The more you pick, the more flowers are produced.

The key to the most succulent runner beans is fortnightly feeding with tomato feed, and watering them every other day. They cannot get enough nutrients and water.

French beans

These come in two forms: dwarf and ordinary. Ordinary French beans should be treated as runner beans (see previous page), except that they need a sunnier spot. They are frost-tender, and don't do so well in cold winds.

Plant dwarf French beans in pots, like broad beans, and then plant them out 20cm apart in late May or early June. They have a long season of producing stringless pods, and need watering and feeding as per runner beans. Harvest as soon as they look ready.

CARROTS

It is possible to have fresh new carrots in the UK at any time of the year by planning ahead and sowing when most of us would not think it possible. Carrots are easy-grow vegetables except in clay, where it is too cold; stony ground when they divide; or too rich ground, where they divide anyway. You might as well join the 'funny-shaped vegetable club', of which we are founder members.

The seeds need a little warmth to get them going. It's best to dig a trench and fill it with a mixture of equal parts of sand and compost. If you cannot do this, then get the hoe out and chop away until you get a crumbly soil. Make a drill (a straight scrape in the soil about 5cm deep) and thinly sow the seeds along it. Cover and water with a rose on your watering can.

As carrots grow they will need to be thinned to plants that are 12cm apart. Keep them 'dry but moist', and every month water with half-strength liquid fertiliser.

The carrot root fly can smell carrots for miles. It skims the soil, and where it finds a member of the carrot family (it attacks parsnips, too) it will lay eggs in the taproot. The grubs then burrow into the carrot, making it completely inedible. The trick to keeping this pest at bay is to put a barrier around the carrots. Carrot fly cannot attain an altitude more than about 40cm, therefore you can easily block its passage onto the plants.

When to sow carrots for a year-round supply

January–February
Sow seeds of Early Nantes or Thumbelina under cloches. These will grow to your first crop around May.

March–April
Sow Baby Bell, Early Nantes or Amsterdam Forcing, which will crop in July. Also sow any of the Chantenay types that will mature in August.

April–May
Sow main-crop carrots Mango, Manchester Table, Jumbo and Resistafly (which implies this has some carrot-fly resistance).

August–September
Repeat sowings of Amsterdam Forcing, Early Nantes, Thumbelina or Autumn King. August-sown plants should be covered with straw in the cold weather, the later ones treated to a cloche. These should provide carrots from Christmas onwards.

CABBAGES, BROCCOLI AND SPROUTS

All the brassicas can be treated in pretty much the same way. They are one of those plant families we simply couldn't live without in our house. They can be cooked, obviously, but go well in salads. There is nothing better than chopping a half cabbage, a little onion, some tomatoes, maybe a little sorrel or rocket, and smothering this with salad dressing – or even just lemon juice.

Cabbages take between 20 and 30 weeks to mature, depending on the variety, and with this in mind you can have fresh plants any time of the year. They prefer a well-dug soil that is reasonably fertile and has lime added. Lime is really important as a deterrent for clubroot. It is possible to grow cabbages in pots, too. If you use a small pot the plant will grow high and not look like a cabbage at all. If you have a large pot – 40cm or more – you will get proper, balled-up cabbages.

How to grow cabbages

There are many ways to grow cabbages. You can grow them outside; the seed is quite hardy and will germinate at low temperatures so long as it isn't actually freezing. However, cabbages suffer from a fungal infection that distorts the roots and stunts the growth of the plant. Clubroot (*Plasmodiophora brassicae*) works mostly on young cabbages and is slowed almost to a standstill in lime.

Fill a drinks cup or an 8cm pot with fresh compost and a tablespoon of lime. Mix well and sow two seeds into each pot. If they are kept warm and watered well you should have germination in about two to three weeks. After five weeks you should have healthily growing plants. In each pot pull out and discard (you can eat them) the slower or weaker-growing plant. Keep the remainder growing in the pots for at least another month, until they've attained a height of about 15cm.

Use a bulb planter to make holes in your soil that are about 40cm apart and about 15cm deep. Line each hole with a lot of lime – about two tablespoons per hole. Then add some fresh compost to the hole, half filling it. Plant in the remainder and firm in well. You can pepper the top of the soil with a little lime. By the time the roots have grown through the fresh compost and the lime the plant will be big enough to cope with the club-root infection, and although you will not always get perfect plants, most of them will be fine.

Keep cabbages weeded with a hoe until the plants are big enough to shade the soil. Cabbages are possibly the best shading plants around. The dying leaves need to be removed, and they should get a feed once every six weeks. This can be liquid or a mulch of well-rotted compost with a little lime in it.

Maintain an even watering regime. If you let them dry and then try to catch up with a good dousing, they will split. You can still eat split cabbages, but they're a good habitat for insects.

Pests

The best way of keeping cabbages clean of insects is to cover them up. You can buy mesh with holes so small aphids cannot get through, but you get a free circulation of air and you can water through it, too.

Cabbage varieties: sowing and harvest times

Autumn Queen Sow in June. Cropping: late autumn/winter.

January King Sow in spring, early under cloches. Harvest from December onwards. Also works for November sowings.

Minicole Sow from April to July. Harvest from October onwards.

Caramba Sow from February indoors to June. Harvest from June to November.

Charmant Sow in spring. Harvest in summer.

Pixie Sow in the summer in succession until autumn. Forms good greens.

Rodeo Red Cabbage Sow in spring, gather in late summer. Pickle for storage.

CAULIFLOWER

Cauliflower is something of a feather in the cap of the gardener. Everyone thinks they are difficult to grow, when in truth they aren't. Treat them just like cabbages (see pages 247–9). Sow in modules or small pots indoors from February to April and plant out into rich soil with a dressing of lime, about 75cm apart when they are about 20cm high. A second sowing in October, kept in a cool greenhouse, can be planted in late April to give summertime cauliflowers.

When planting them out, firm them in with your heel. If you sow every fortnight from February to April, you can have plants ready for picking from August to October. It's important to avoid having a lot of heads ripen at the same time, although you can freeze them.

BROCCOLI AND SPROUTS

Treat in the same way as cabbages (see pages 247–9) but it is really important to heel the plants in so that they are firmly embedded. Otherwise the rocking caused by the wind will either force the buttons to open or the plants to run to seed.

SWEDES

This member of the brassica family is grown for its root. Where would we be without carrot and swede, boiled, mixed up and mashed to a paste? They are sown like cabbages (see pages 247–9) and should be treated in the same way, including planting them with lime. They stay in the ground a little later, normally during the first week in June. Apart from watering in times of drought, there is little else to do with them. The swollen roots appear above the soil and they can stay there right through the year. Frosts make them a little sweeter, if anything. It is an easy-to-grow crop – well worth the springtime sowing.

CELERY

If you want good soup, you need good celery. It's a fairly easy crop to grow, though hungry. Dig a trench at least 45cm deep and fill the bottom half with well-rotted manure, then fill the top with rich compost. Sow in modules indoors in March and at room temperature, or you won't get them to germinate. Thin to at east one plant per module. In May transplant them to the trench, about 45cm apart. Keep them moist and feed with tomato food, or some other liquid fertiliser, once a month. Harvest as you need them.

CELERIAC

This is an interesting plant. It has a swollen root like a potato with a celery flavour. It can be boiled and mashed (yummy), sliced and fried in butter (yummier) and added to other vegetables in a roast.

Celeriac is easy to grow, but you do need soil that has been previously manured for a hungrier crop – potatoes are ideal. Sow in 8cm pots indoors in March and transplant in late May to their final growing positions. Keep them moist but free-draining, and weed them well. They will be ready in September. Don't grow too many; they will keep in the soil until the first frosts. They don't store well, so are better harvested and eaten straight away.

LEEKS

Leeks are fascinating plants to grow because they are very unusual plants. They are members of the allium family, whose relatives are onions, garlic, chives and shallots. Once transplanted into their final positions, leeks will happily stay in the ground right through the winter, resisting both storms and frost. As long as the soil around them is firm, they'll be fine, and they should be harvested when you need them, usually from October onwards. You can grow them in pots at any time of the year, but they become 'baby leeks', never attaining a size bigger than a fat finger. They make great layers in vegetable tureens with peppers and potatoes.

Start by sowing in March in trays of compost. If you can get a deep container, around 20cm, you'll be able to grow them on until they are pencil-sized. Simply sprinkle the compost with the seeds, cover with compost, firm them in a little and water. Use a bulb planter to create holes that are 15cm deep and about 24cm apart. Rows should be around 50cm apart.

Take the young leeks, cut off all but the last 4cm of root and trim the top of the leaves by the same amount. You now have what looks like a bunch of prepared salad onions. Drop one plant into each hole, then fill the hole with water. It doesn't matter if the water washes a little soil over the roots; all you need to make sure of is that the plants are upright. From this position they will happily grow to maturity.

Care

Leeks do especially well if planted where a previous crop has received a heavy load of manure, or following a crop that adds nitrogen to the soil, such as beans. Potash deficiency can lead to increased fungal infection, so to combat this, water the plants with some organic fertiliser once a month during the growing period. The growing leeks will expand into the hole, and rain and general watering will eventually fill the rest of the space with soil. By October, make sure the leeks are firmed into the soil with the judicious use of the heel of your boot. This will stop them being blown about by the winter winds.

Leeks are really hardy and you can leave them in the ground for as long as you need. The rain splashes soil around them, however, so for perfect leeks you need to protect them. Use cut-out drainpipes, which also serve to blanch (whiten) the lower part.

Onions

If you want the best onions in the world, have a bonfire on your plot, mix all the wood ash with the soil using a fork, then hoe it to make a fine, crumbly mixture and grow your onions in this. Traditionally, onions were sown on Christmas Day, but most people are usually too busy. Sow in modules or trays of compost and grow them until they're around 12cm tall. These plants can be transplanted in April, around 30cm apart.

By far the easiest way to grow onions is to plant onion sets. These are little bulbs that have been heat-treated so they will never run to seed. Push the bulbs, flat-end down, into small holes you've prepared with a dibber. They should be around 30cm apart and the rows should be 45cm apart. The variety Sturon is most popular – and very inexpensive.

They like a feed of liquid fertiliser once a month until August, by which time they should be almost ready to harvest. The leaves fall over and you need to lift them using a fork – don't just pull them up. This is usually done by the end of August or the first week in September.

Japanese onions Yellow Express should be sown in July or sets planted in August. These will overwinter and give you a crop in May or June. Leave the bulbs to harden – a process known as 'curing' – in the open air, but away from the rain. The outer leaves will become leathery and you can then store them. It is best to store them on a tray in a dry, cool position.

Peas

There are lots of pea types, each to be treated more or less in the same way. Try sugar snap and mangetout as well the old favourite, Kelvedon Wonder. But you could also splash out a little: where would cold Lancashire evenings be without black-eyed peas and plenty of vinegar and pepper?

Peas are easy to grow in all soils except clay. They refuse to germinate in cold, clay soil and that's that. In clay soils you have to dig a trench about 30cm deep and 30cm wide and fill it with compost.

You can grow peas in a cold greenhouse. Sow seeds in 8cm pots in December and let them grow right through to the spring, when they should be planted out into the sunniest part of the garden. Simply knock the pot off and plant the whole rootball into some well-dug soil. You'll have peas in late May or early June.

Start sowing directly into the ground in March. Plant peas in well-dug soil about 5cm deep and about 15cm apart. Repeat this every two weeks until July and you will have a succession of fresh peas from July to September. The variety Kelvedon Wonder grows well in all parts of the country.

POTATOES

There are so many potato varieties and their growing season is so long that it makes one wonder why we don't have potato connoisseurs in this country in the same way there are experts on truffles or pastry. Potatoes have a huge range of flavours and are simply wonderful, from the very early Lady Christl to the good old King Edward. Not only do you have a huge variety of flavours, but you get a lot of variance in texture, too. A Pentland Javelin not only tastes different but feels different to a Jersey; a Pink Fir Apple looks different, too; long, knobbly, impossible-to-peel, yet with a flavour that makes planting them so much worth the effort.

There are basically two types of potato: waxy and floury. Floury potatoes are used for mashing, frying or roasting. Waxy potatoes are used wherever the texture of the flesh needs to remain intact: for salad potatoes, boiling and making dishes such as *rösti*. Floury potatoes are used where the cell walls burst, releasing starch that crisps up in salty fat, making them ideal for chips and roasted potatoes.

Potatoes by type

WAXIEST
Nadine, Pink Fir Apple, Cara, Marfona, Home Guard, Sharp's Express, Estima, Wilja, Saxon, Nicola, Charlotte, Kestrel, Maris Peer, Maris Piper, Romano, Desire, King Edward, Sante

FLOURIEST
Golden Wonder

To have fresh potatoes almost all the year round, you do not need a lot of space, but the more you have, the better. You can grow potatoes in pots and containers at the kitchen door, in sacks in the yard or garden, in the greenhouse and polytunnel and on the allotment. Almost invariably the same conditions are important. Potatoes need moisture, lots of nutrients and a frost-free environment. If these three conditions are met, you can grow potatoes any time of the year. Traditionally potatoes are buried in the ground in spring and dug up in the summer or early autumn. Since more of us have greenhouses and polytunnels, however, so it is possible to grow potatoes in tubs in July and August, transferring them to the greenhouse in September and have a crop from November through to January and even beyond.

The 'hungry gap' for potatoes is February to the end of May. This is plugged by using stored old potatoes that were cropped in September. Floury potatoes keep very well in dry conditions.

How long to grow?
'First early' potatoes need between 12 to 15 weeks from the day you put them in the ground to produce a crop. Traditionally first earlies are planted no later than St Patrick's Day (17 March). If you use the ultra-early Lady Christl, you will have a crop on 17 June.

Basically you could plant potatoes every two weeks from 17 March right through to the end of June (though the end of May is preferable), by which time you should have the maincrop potatoes in place. These need 20 weeks to reach maturity, and you should have a crop in late October.

FIRST EARLY VARIETIES (PLANT BY MID-MARCH)
Maris Peer, Home Guard, Arran Pilot, Pentland Javelin, Rocket, Pink Fir Apple

SECOND EARLY VARIETIES (PLANT BY MID-APRIL)
Kestrel, Wilja, Estima, Osprey, Nadine

MAINCROP VARIETIES (PLANT BY THE END OF MAY)
Admiral, Cara, Eden, Maris Piper, King Edward

Preparation
Growing potatoes in the ground is a question of preparation. During the winter you need to incorporate a lot of well-rotted manure, at least a couple of wheelbarrows full for every row of potatoes. (A row is 10m long and 1m wide.)

Buy new potatoes each year; never save old ones because they build up disease. Also, buy specific varieties – do not rely on supermarket spuds to do well. Go to the garden centre, send off for a catalogue or buy online.

Chitting
This is the natural process whereby the 'eye', or growing bud, on the tuber starts to grow – a process triggered by a number of factors. Simply leave your potatoes in a light, airy place and the buds will burst into life. Even if they haven't, plant according to their variety.

Open a trench
Dig the soil so it is light and fluffy to a depth of about 75cm. A rotavator is best for this if you have one, but a spade will do. Then make a trench about 35cm deep. Place your potatoes in

the trench at intervals of about 1m. Fill in the trench and water lightly. This will encourage the potatoes to start growing in earnest.

Each row of potatoes should be around 1m from the next. You can then plant a 'catch crop' between the rows, such as radishes and marigolds: plant one for salads, the other just because they're really pretty!

When the potato shoots appear above the ground and attain a height of about 30cm, draw some soil around the shoots with a hoe. The idea is to make sure any tubers do not appear out of the soil. If they see sunlight, tubers will become green, with an associated increase in poisonous chemicals.

Care

There should be plenty of manure, and therefore nutrients, in the ground. As they grow, potatoes need water, so never let the crop dry out, but similarly do not let them become waterlogged. Water at the base of the plants to avoid blight and other fungal infections and try not to let the plants become too bushy, trapping moisture in the air around the leaves.

Pests

There are lots of pests, but two are worse than others: blight and slugs. Blight can be treated, but it is best avoided. It is a fungal infection that needs warmth and moisture. If you make sure the leaves are well-ventilated, you will probably avoid blight. Since blight normally comes after mid-July, early potatoes do not suffer.

You can, of course, grow blight-resistant strains, which include:

- Red Cara (maincrop)
- Cara, Sarpo Axona, Sarpo Mira, Valor, Verity (all late maincrop)

Possibly the best way of treating potatoes for slugs is to use parasitic nematode worms, which you can buy from garden centres or specialist suppliers. A product such as Nemaslug is dissolved in water and sprinkled on the soil at a particular time of year. It does work, but is quite expensive and possibly needs a repeat application.

Christmas potatoes

You can use this method at any time of the year; it works best with early potatoes. You need a large pot, preferably a plastic one because they are lighter and you have to move these around. Make sure the pot is well-drained.

Half fill the pot with good, rich compost and lay two potato tubers in the compost. Fill this with compost and water. When the leaves appear, water weekly, more often if the compost is dry in hot weather. Once a fortnight add some liquid fertiliser to the water.

When the frosts are due, bring them into a cool but frost-free greenhouse and maintain the regime, but water slightly less to avoid fungal disease. Never let the compost become completely dry.

You can harvest any time after 15 weeks, so if you plant the first week in August, you can harvest in the last week in October, and so on. For Christmas potatoes you need them in the pots by the third week in August.

RHUBARB

One cannot describe the flavour of rhubarb except to say it is a complete surprise. It is packed with sugar and the acid flavour comes from a number of chemicals, one of them – oxalic acid – being poisonous. For this reason, do not pick and eat rhubarb from the garden after June and never eat the leaves.

Rhubarb comes as a small plant called a crown. Enrich the soil with well-rotted manure in December and plant the crown about 30cm deep in January. This will push out shoots in April and you will have a young plant in May.

Do not take any stems in the first year. The plant dies back in the winter. When this happens, remove the dead leaves and compost them. Then give a good mulch of well-rotted compost.

The following spring you'll have more stems. Take about a third of them once they are as fat as two fingers. Repeat the winter feeding and replace your stock every four years.

SALAD

Lettuce, rocket, beets, radish… all of these can be treated in the same way, really. In essence you plonk the seed into the ground and they grow. After you have waited as long as you can, harvest them for salads.

Start sowing salad leaves as early as April, and every couple of weeks sow some more somewhere else. Thin out your seedlings so the mature plants end up being a hands-width apart. These instructions go for all salad leaves, including beets and chard. The same goes for radishes, too: just bung them in.

If you sow in succession from April to the end of August, you will have salad out in the open most of the year. From September to December you can sow indoors in a frost-free greenhouse and have fresh salad for the rest of the year.

All the care they need is regular water, protection from insects and rabbits (and cats in our garden), for which I use mesh. Slugs are another problem (see page 254). At around six weeks, give them a feed of liquid fertiliser.

TOMATOES

There are so many varieties of tomatoes that you can usually get a good crop both indoors and outdoors. Two old varieties, Money Maker and Gardener's Delight, will always be profitable and yield a crop in any of the British weather conditions. You can buy a lot of Italian tomatoes these days; Pomodoro is a current favourite. It is surprising that many Italian tomatoes are grown in conditions not unlike the UK, but high up in the mountains.

Sow in 8cm pots in March indoors at around 20°C and grow until they can be potted on at around 20cm high. From there you can transfer them to growbags indoors or outdoors. The outdoor ones are best in large 45cm pots, which you can easily move around. You can put them into growbags in the greenhouse in May. Indoor tomatoes can be put into the greenhouse in May, but I usually wait until late June before putting outdoor tomatoes in position. They need a sunny aspect.

All tomatoes need support, which can be in the form of canes (watch your eyes when you water them) or strings. You should not let them dry out, and always water them uniformly. Leaving them a week and then giving them a soaking to make up for the drought will lead to black fruit and a condition called blossom end rot. From June onwards feed with tomato fertiliser once a week.

Ripening

This happens from August onwards. By the end of August remove all the leaves from the plant. This cuts down the chance of disease, and speeds ripening. Any unripe fruit can be used in chutney – trying to forcibly ripen them (for example, by using rotting fruit) makes for poor flavour.

TURNIPS

No vegetable is easier to grow than the turnip. Neither is there a better vegetable to roast: you can really taste the earth it grew in! Turnips can be grown at almost any time of the year, in soil or in containers of compost. They need a little warmth to get the seed to germinate, but following that, they need minimal care.

Sow directly into the place they are to grow from spring onwards. Hoe the ground so that you have a fine, crumbly soil, and make a scrape (called a drill) that is 5cm deep and as long as you need. Sow lightly in this, cover and water. Within 10 days you will have seedlings, which you thin by taking out every second one. Repeat the thinning process every couple of weeks until you have about 15cm between each turnip. Otherwise water when dry, but basically leave them alone. Harvest when they are cricket-ball-sized.

You can sow in a container at any time of the year, in a cool greenhouse. The only months you're not likely to have fresh turnips are January and February.

Growing Common Edible Herbs

When we think about the use of herbs in cooking, we automatically think of French or Italian cuisine, believing subconsciously that our own cooking is plain, simple or even bland. It hasn't always been this way, however. From medieval times onward, what we would now consider herbs were the most important plants in the kitchen garden. The potager was created as a way of growing herbs and pulses in the most space-economical way possible, and in an age where there were no chemicals, clever positioning of plants made them less prone to insect attack.

Historically, herbs have long been a major part of English cooking. Their demise has been caused in part by supermarkets and prepared food. The TV dinner, fast foods and convenience kitchens designed for warming up food wrapped in a tin have all made us uncertain about how to use fresh or even dried herbs.

Growing herbs at home is the only way to get fresh, full, real flavours. The herbs you buy in shops have been under artificial (and frequently inadequate) light for a long time, and they are not as power-packed with flavour as they should be. Yet they can sometimes be hardy, so you could even buy all the herbs from the supermarket and plant them out into pots, containers and beds to populate your herb garden.

Choosing and growing herbs

The desire to have an enormous herb garden is sometimes more vanity than practicality. Realistically, we use only a few herbs very often. Others are still worth growing as they are used regularly – around once a month. Fennel, for example, is one of the herbs many gardeners wouldn't be without, yet it can be limited in its usage. We hardly ever use fennel in cooking, for example, unless we have some fish to smoke, particularly sea bass. Then we take a wok and fill it with fennel and on top of this, over a grill, we put the fish. Then we ignite the fennel and it cooks the fish, giving it an interesting flavour as it burns.

Most herbs do well in pots of compost. You can sow directly into fairly large pots – say 20cm in diameter. The advantage of this is that you can move the pots around the garden or patio, into the sunlight or away from the wind.

Some herbs, like mint, need to be grown in pots unless you don't mind them growing out of control and taking over the whole garden. One minute you have a small mint plant in a bed and the next you cannot get to the front door without falling into a minty death trap. You can bury pots in a bed if you like, so that the plants appear to be in the ground.

Anise
Use the leaves and the seeds of this plant, which have a strong aniseed flavour.

Sow
In a 45cm pot filled with 25 percent sand and 75 percent compost, with a handful of grit to increase drainage. Sow in April, a few seeds per pot.

Care
Use leaves in year 1, and let it seed in year 2. Keep the seeds in envelopes.

Basil
Sow
In pots in April. Maintain a temperature of 15°C. The seedlings will emerge after a fortnight.

Care
Keep moist but not too wet. You can prolong its life through the winter by bringing it indoors, as basil will be destroyed by frost. Feed with liquid fertiliser once a month at the base.

Borage
Sow
In March in modules or trays of ordinary compost. Prick out into 8cm pots and pot on until they are in 30cm pots.

Care
These are happy plants to grow, as they do well in all circumstances. Feed monthly with a liquid feed.

Caraway
Sow
Sprinkle a few seeds in 30cm pots in September. In April, thin to one per pot, and transplant the thinnings to other 30cm pots.

Care
Keep caraway watered and fed fortnightly. Keep frost-free during the following winter and water less in the winter, too. The following summer the plants will produce seed, which may be collected and used in cooking.

Chamomile
Sow
In spring, scatter seeds into any bit of soil you need it, in the cracks between pavements... anywhere, really. Sprinkle so much seed that you don't have to think about the plant again.

Care
None. Simply sow and forget. It looks after itself.

Chives
Sow
In April, liberally into 30cm pots. Really cram them in, cover with compost, firm in and water.

Care
Keep moist, and feed with liquid fertiliser monthly. Cut with scissors – they grow back.

Dill
Sow
In spring in 8cm pots. This will usually do fine if you keep it moist, but it is probably better bought from the supermarket as plants and potted into larger containers.

Care
Water and feed monthly. Dill isn't hardy, so you need fresh supplies each year.

Marjoram
Sow
In April, in 8cm pots. Transplant to 20cm pots.

Care
Needs to be well-fed at least once every three weeks with a tomato feed. Keep moist but not wet. In September, bring into a cool greenhouse, which will extend its life until late November. Grow fresh plants each year.

Lavender
Sow
Probably best to buy plants and transplant them into their growing place.

Care
Keep moist and feed monthly. Prune in winter to keep the plant's shape, and encourage growth. More of a haircut than a full-blown prune, though!

Mustard
Sow
In April in trays and simply let them grow for mustard greens.

Care
Transplant a few plants into 15cm pots and let them go to seed. They ripen in September.

Mint
Sow
In large pots in April indoors and set them out in the garden in June. Possibly best to buy from supermarkets – or specialist suppliers, where you will get a huge number of varieties – and transplant.

Care
Start some plants fresh each year. They will come back themselves, but they tend to get a little woody and scruffy.

Parsley
Sow
On a tray in April and transplant the seedlings to 8cm pots when big enough to handle.

Care
Keep warm and moist and it will grow quickly. You can transplant them from 8cm pots into final growing positions in June.

Rosemary
Sow
Can be difficult to germinate so is much better bought as plants. You can take cuttings almost any time of the year and pot in compost.

Care
Keep out of the wind. Don't let it be too moist, but never let it become bone-dry. Feed once during the summer.

Sage

Sow

Grow in 30cm pots from plants bought from suppliers or supermarkets.

Care

Sage is quite hardy. Give it a good feed in the growing period and mulch with rich compost in autumn and spring.

Thyme

Sow

In seeds in March indoors. Sow in modules and transplant when the plants are 8cm tall. Put them into 15cm pots.

Care

Make sure they're neither too wet or dry. Feed monthly and replenish your stock every two years.

Fruit in Season

Growing fruit can become something of a passion, especially if you have a polytunnel or greenhouse to play with. Some fruits are grown like treats around the garden. Strawberries, for example, turn up in the flower borders; it's really wonderful to be working under a hot sun in the border somewhere to find a ripe strawberry to pop into your mouth.

The big thing to remember about fruits is that as soon as you pick them they begin to deteriorate. Some – blackberries picked in woodland, for example – are so different when you get them home than when you picked them. It is little wonder that many fruits are packed in plastic to keep them somewhere near fresh.

Growing fruit is often a little more involved than vegetables, and you have to compete with millions, even billions of other species that want your fruit as much as you do. Yet growing some fruit, even if it's only the odd strawberry, is one of the greatest experiences on offer to mankind because you can pop out into the garden from June to November and have something completely delicious to eat!

Apples and Pears

Whatever is said for apples is also true for pears, so the two can dealt with in the same section here. You don't need a lot of space to grow apples and pears; all you need is a wall. Tie branches to wires and train them to produce fruit in a long, thin line. And you can always find the right tree for you because apples are grafted onto various roots that control the overall size of the final tree. These 'controlling roots' are called rootstocks and come in various forms.

Rootstock	Height
M27	1.2m
M26	2m
MM106	3–4m
M25	5m

So you can grow apples on plants ranging from those that are good in containers to huge trees as big as a house. It is true that climate has a role in apple production and every county has its own varieties.

Container verses bare-rooted
Apples come in two forms: bare-rooted or containered. Bare-rooted plants come wrapped in wet newspaper and must be planted in winter, when the tree is dormant. Containered plants have a ball of earth around the roots and can be planted anytime. Consider three things when you are planting your tree:

Site
Apples need to be protected from strong winds, and they need good sun. If you are able to plant windbreak hedges or build a fence, all the better.

Soil
Needs to be rich and full of nutrients. Dig the soil well and incorporate plenty of rich compost.

Drainage
Apples like dry feet. Make sure your soil is free-draining. You can increase the drainage by digging 75cm down and adding a good 10cm of grit to the bottom of the hole.

When planting, dig a large hole, at least twice the volume of the rootball or one and a half times as deep as the bare-rooted root. Fill the bottom with rich compost. Drive a stake in at 45° angle before you plant the tree. Put the tree in place so that the scar (where the tree is grafted onto the rootstock) is just above the ground by about 2cm.

Fill in with rich soil/compost mix and firm in well. Use a rubber tree support to fix the tree to the stake. Water well. Mulch the tree with compost, then keep replacing this mulch as it is rained in. Do not let the mulch touch the stem.

Do not take any fruit until the third year. You are best taking fruit off as it appears in years one and two so that the tree can build up its strength.

Apricots
We have long grown apricots in this country because they are fairly easy, and it has to be said that an apricot grown in the garden bears no resemblance to those bought in the shops – the former are so much better.

In the south of England you can grow apricots outside, and since they are quite hardy they will grow well. In the north, however, the driving, cold winds of winter wear them down, so it is much better to put them in a polytunnel.

Plant them a mix of good soil enriched with a few spades of good compost. Prune the plant in the early years to get a good shape, but apart from that it only needs trimming to keep its growth under control.

Pollination is difficult. Apricots flower in spring and there are likely to be few insects to do the job, so lightly dust each flower with a feather and you will get good fruit set. The variety 'Moor Park' is the bog-standard apricot that does well and can be relied on to produce fruit all around the country.

Blackcurrants

There is nothing more wonderful on the plot, when digging the soil in early spring, than to be distracted by the smell of blackcurrants. There are no leaves, just leaf buds, but the aroma sent into the air by the rising sap pervades the whole garden. It is worth growing them just for this phenomenon.

Blackcurrants need rich soil and good sun. Dig a 60cm x 60cm hole that is 60cm deep. Plant blackcurrants 1.2m apart. The best time to do this is in the winter when the plant is dormant. They will quickly grow to fill in the gaps and you will end up with a really wonderful, fruity hedge. The variety Ben Lomond can be relied on to produce a full crop in any part of the country.

Care

In the winter, firm blackcurrants in with your boot and give them a mulch of good compost. A feed of liquid fertiliser in the spring, once the leaves have set, will give the plant a good boost. Net the bushes once the fruit is set because the birds will eat them all. Collect fruit in summer.

Pruning

In the second winter trim away dead branches and ones that are crossing. Then take 20 percent of the inside of the branches so that the plant opens out to encourage air ventilation, which will in turn encourage greater disease resistance.

Melons

The summer is not worth its name without a good melon from the garden. You need really well-draining soil for melons and wide beds, at least 2m wide. The bed should have a mound in it so that you can plant your melons and have the leaves and fruit falling along the slope.

Start your seeds in an 8cm pot in April; water and keep it at room temperature. Discard the slowest-growing plant. Transplant to their growing position that has been prepared with lots of rich compost. Each plant should be 1.5m apart. This should be done at the end of May or early June, when the frosts have passed. If it's cold and wet, put a cloche over the plants until the weather becomes hotter.

Get as much heat into the ground as you can: covering with black plastic helps. Mulch around the plants with good compost. Some people cover the soil with newspaper and then cover this with grass cuttings which, as they rot down, release nutrients into the soil. Feed with tomato feed once a week. Above all, melons need warmth, so if summer is poor, cover them with a cloche.

Harvesting
Your melons are ready when they are 'slippy'. This doesn't mean when they're wet, only that when they fall off their stems easily, they are ready. Leave them a day or so after harvest if you like that aromatic flavour.

Raspberries and Blackberries
There are millions of these plants. They are the most permissive plants in the garden, forming all kinds of different varieties, too numerous to mention. They are usually grown as canes that need good, rich soil that is moisture-retentive but not waterlogged.

Dig a trench 40cm deep by 30cm wide. Incorporate a lot of well-rotted manure and compost into this and build a frame to support the canes.

Plant them in winter 40cm apart and firm them in well. Cut them to 15cm high – an important step for good growth. In the first year pinch off any fruit. They produce fruit on this year's shoots that come from last year's branches.

Summer-fruiting raspberries need to be pruned by cutting last year's branches to 20cm from the ground. Autumn-fruiting ones need the branches that have just fruited cut to 20cm.

Strawberries
Strawberries are tough little plants that cope with frost very easily unless they have young flowers in place. They produce lots of fruit, and get their name from the practice of laying straw under the fruit to keep them clean of mud. Straw also keeps the snails off.

Strawberries are usually sold as new plants. Perhaps the very best time to plant them is April and May, which gives them a good growing period before having to face a winter. Plantings in September also do well.

The plants need to be watered every couple of days when first planted, but after a couple of weeks they should be fine. Do not water so much as to cause puddles. Once established, the plants start to reproduce by flowers and runners.

Runners are like rhizomes that appear above the soil. At intervals of about 40cm, a little strawberry plant will appear. Anchor this plant into a pot of compost and you will soon have another genetically identical plant. This is the best way of replacing stock. For maximum fruit production, cut the runners off.

Planting
Plant strawberries so the lowest of the 'branches' is under the soil. Do not bury the central bud. Firm it in well with the fingers and give it a good drink. If you plant them high they will fall over in the wind; too low and they will rot.

There are so many varieties available. Try Flamenco for plants that bear fruit all the summer. Amelia will happily produce plants that give fruit into September and even beyond if you cover with a cloche. Marshmarvel will provide a crop as early as late May in some parts of the country.

Strawberries get tired after two years of production. Replace these with new plants taken from runners.

It is true to say that every season of the year has something new when it comes to brewing beer or fermenting wine. Wine is supposed to be too delicate a drink for such a rough word as 'brewing'; essentially, however, the processes are the same. Provide as much sugar as you can to feed the yeast, exclude as much oxygen as you are able and you end up with alcohol in water solution. The flavour has nothing to do with this process except for the fact that the alcohol reacts with the molecules in the bottle to create subtle differences – some more subtle than others. It is surprising how slow this process can be. Most of the time, we expect chemistry to be all but instantaneous, but in a wine bottle, the reactions can take months and even years to complete.

You can use almost anything to give your wine or beer flavour. Beer is usually flavoured with barley and hops, boiled together to dissolve all the sugar in the malted barley. The hops give a bitter flavour to the mash, which, when strained and ready for brewing, is known as a 'wort'. Wine – good wine – is nearly all fruit juice and usually has a lot more sugar in the mix than beer. Consequently, wine can be really high in alcohol at 12 percent by volume (abv), whereas beer is usually less than 6 percent abv.

The aim of this chapter is to give you enough confidence to make wine and beer from almost anything, according to what is around in the season.

Seasonal Wine & Beer

Making Wine According to Season

Some books include recipes that call for obscure ingredients, and you can't imagine why they were included or how they make the wine any tastier. Other recipes for wine are actually something else entirely: for example, dandelion wine that is more or less orange juice or grape juice, and when you drink it, you wonder at the dandelion content. It's best not be a slave to books but to remember a couple of basic principles and let the yeast do the rest. If you end up with good wine, it is because the ingredients were good and the technique used is very simple. Master that, and the rest is easy.

What winemaking is all about

Yeast can live by breaking down sugar to give off carbon dioxide and water. When bread is rising before it is baked, it is because of this process. Take the air away, however, and yeast doesn't die because it has a clever trick: it changes its metabolism so that instead of metabolising sugar to give off carbon dioxide, it makes its own oxygen from the sugar, a process that gives off alcohol. Then it respires in the normal way with the oxygen it has made for itself to give off carbon dioxide, too.

The problem for the yeast is that alcohol is poisonous, and as the brew gets stronger, the increasing alcohol concentration increases and the yeast slows down until it can no longer survive in the liquid. This happens at around 15 percent alcohol concentration, but the yeast slows down considerably long before then.

Wine is spoiled when there are too many dead yeast cells in the liquid. Part of the winemaking art is getting rid of all these cells, which fall to the bottom of the vessel and are called lees. This is done by repeatedly pouring off (racking) the clearer liquid at the top of the demijohn and letting the poured wine continue its fermentation. The wine is finished when the airlock stops bubbling.

Basic winemaking equipment

Traditionally the demijohn, which holds a gallon of liquid, is required for fermenting, but you also need another one to receive the poured-off wine once this first fermentation is complete. You therefore need a hose to transfer the wine from one demijohn to another by siphoning.

Then you need a way of expelling air from the top of the bottles, which is done by fitting an airlock in a bung on top of the demijohn. Put water in the airlock and it bubbles away, telling you that the yeast is doing its job. That is all you need in terms of equipment. Use three senses to see if wine is ready: taste, sight more than anything else, and smell.

Clean everything

It goes without saying that all equipment used in winemaking or brewing should be spotless. Old-fashioned stone demijohns can be boiled, but the thin glass ones cannot cope with hot liquids at all, so you need to use sterilising tablets. These work well, but they do release chemicals into the planet – even though they came from the planet in the first place. Don't forget to sterilise the bungs and everything associated with the winemaking process, as well.

The basics

If you make a gallon of juice, or flavoured water with any flavourings you like, and dissolve a kilo of sugar in it, a teaspoon of winemaking yeast, and a vitamin C tablet, in a fortnight you will have a drink that is about 6–10 percent abv. When the yeast is dead completely, the drink will be around 14 percent abv. We are not talking *grand cru* vintages here; just plain, simple, delicious country wines, brewed (fermented) until the airlock stops bubbling.

When the bubbles stop

Ideally, you need a stone floor for this. Wash your hands and siphon off the wine into a second vessel, being careful not to take in all the lees on the bottom. Before refitting the bung and airlock, give the wine a vigorous shaking. (Put your hand over the bottle lip to prevent spillage.) All the gas will escape and you should repeat this until you can get no more gas out of the bottle. This way, the particles in the wine fall to the bottom of the bottle more easily. Put the bottle on a stone floor because vibrations from people walking around on floorboards can actually mix the wine.

When the wine clears, resiphon and repeat until you have a clear container of wine. You can now bottle this. The screwtop wine bottles that are around these days are ideal for recycling for this purpose, or you can cork bottles in the traditional way. Use a proper bottle corker, though – a hammer often ends in tragedy – and don't forget to sterilise the bottles and the corks.

Leave the wine alone for as long as you can. Sometimes we've simply used the demijohn to pour from, but the longer you can leave it alone, the better.

Making the juice

There are a number of simple ways to remove the flavour and essential oils from the materials used in making wine and beer.

Spurging

Use this for flowers, oats and grain. Spurging is where you put the material – say, for example, some elderflower heads, beautifully white in early summer – and douse it with boiling water. The juice is poured off through a muslin once cool. You usually only use as much water as you would finally need in the fermentation vessel: 4.5 litres for a demijohn, but if you're going to brew beer you will have to boil the materials for several minutes, then add cold water to the liquor (now called a wort).

Steeping
Use this for oats and some grain, dandelion flowers and most leaves, such as mint. It is like spurging in that you pour boiling water over the ingredient, except you leave it to soak in the slowly cooling water for 24 hours. The liquor is then strained off as normal.

Crushing
Use crushing for all forms of soft fruit. Wash your fruit and wrap it in muslin, tying it off so that you have a large bundle. Spurge this with boiling water, just enough to cover, and use a rolling pin or crusher to smash the contents of the bag. Be careful not to burn yourself if the water is still hot. Once the liquid is cold, squeeze out the last dregs of flavour from the parcel into your liquid.

Pulping and crushing
Use this method with hard fruit such as apples, as well as with stems and roots. Put the cleaned ingredient into a food blender, blitz it, then empty the contents into muslin, which is placed inside a screw-crusher, if you have one. Clamp on the follower (the bit that does the crushing) and turn the screw until the juice stops running. If you don't have a crusher, then simply pummel it as described below.

S EASONAL   W INES
The following winemaking suggestions assume you're making 4.5 litres of wine and using 1kg of ordinary white sugar. You need a food-grade tub (sterile), muslin to collect the fruit in and to strain all the juice out – squeezing hard with clean hands. Otherwise, a kettle of boiling water poured over the fruit, mashed with a potato masher, is all you need. Put the fruit in the muslin first and give it a good pummelling, then add the sugar to the juice and leave it to cool before pouring it into the demijohn.

Spring
Dandelion
This takes a while: use 500g flower petals in a pan, add a couple of pints of water, bring to the boil, allow to cool, strain and top up with apple juice.

Parsnip
Chop up 3kg of parsnips and pour a kettle of boiling water over them. Leave to steep overnight. Squeeze out the last bit of liquid from them. For more flavour, grate the roots.

Late Spring
Elderflower
Use about 3–4 heads as big as your hand.

Early Summer
Rhubarb
Makes a tart wine that eventually tastes like very dry sherry. You need about 750g of rhubarb.

Summer
Barley
This is a good one. Use 500g barley and 500g chopped raisins. Add the water and soak overnight. Strain the juice for making the wine.

Carrot
Chop up 3kg of carrots and pour a kettle of boiling water over them. Leave to steep overnight. Squeeze out the last bit of liquid from the carrots.

Late Summer
Blackberry
It takes ages to collect 2kg blackberries – but it's well worth it.

Damson
Use 3kg damsons – or plums – and leave overnight before setting off.

Elderberry
Use 1kg elderberries, 2 litres of water and 2 litres of diluted blackcurrant juice or 2kg blackcurrants.

Late Summer/Autumn
Rosehip
You don't need vitamin C in this as there is already lots in the rosehips. Use 1.5kg rosehips and a kettle of boiling water – leave for an hour, then make the wine.

Early Autumn
Mead
Use 1kg honey to water, and 2 cups of lemon juice. It is better if you use a white-wine concentrate kit. Leave to mature for hundreds of years (well, at least two!).

Autumn
Apple Wine
Use 3kg apples, pulped in a food processor. A cup of lemon juice prevents browning.

Sloes
Use 2kg of sloes, add boiled water, and mash. Decant, make the wine and mature it at least a year.

Making Beer

If you can make wine, you can make beer, although you need a different set of tools. In student days we used to make brown ale in dustbins. There are some problems with brewing with a larger amount of liquid, particular with the amount of oxygen in the vessel. The thing about brewing with hops is that there is a lot of protein in the liquid, and this forms a 'scum' or froth of carbon dioxide bubbles. This covering at the top of the liquid is what stops fresh oxygen getting into the liquid, and therefore the yeast will use up the oxygen in the water quite quickly.

All of which means that beer is usually lower in alcohol, quite apart from the fact that we add less sugar compared with the amount of liquid in the vessel. It is not possible to use demijohns to make beer; you need at least a 25-litre container, usually in the form of a plastic tub with a sealable lid. You can buy plastic barrels with taps built into the base. These taps are a couple of inches above the bottom of the barrel, allowing the beer to be poured off without disturbing the settled yeast.

Brewing from a kit

By far the best way of starting to brew beer is to buy a kit. You get everything you need to make 25 litres, including a simple wort (brewing liquid); you only have to add the sugar. Dissolve the wort in the appropriate amount of water, according to the instructions, and add the required amount of sugar. Add the yeast and tighten the lid in place and a couple of weeks later you'll have beer.

It is a good idea when brewing beer to use glucose rather than ordinary white sugar. It gives it a 'professional' beery flavour.

Altering a brew kit

You can easily change the brew kit to make some wonderful beers. Using honey instead of sugar is a great idea, especially if you buy a 'bitter' kit – you get a darker, golden beer with a deeper flavour. Since honey is only 80 percent sugar, for every kilo of sugar the instructions suggest, you need to add 1.2kg of honey.

Dark beers, brown ale and so on, are further enhanced by 50 percent sugar and 50 percent dark treacle to give them a burned, nutty flavour.

Brewing from scratch

You can make small batches of beer from your own bought hops and malt. You can grow these hops yourself, and there are people out there with a garden large enough to accommodate them, but mostly they are bought from home-brew shops. It is quite easy, and the house gets a wonderful aroma. In essence, it is a case of boiling the hops in a pan and then making up the resulting liquid to the required volume.

You will need
    4.5 litres water
    1kg dark dried malt extract
    450g light dried malt extract
    125g Goldings hops
    1kg brown sugar
    1.4kg white sugar
    1 tablespoon beer yeast

Pour the water into a large pan, add the malt extract and hops and bring to a boil. Turn down the heat and simmer for 30 minutes, then strain into the fermenting vessel. Wash the hops out with a couple of kettles of boiling water. Make up to the 20 litres with cold water and dissolve the sugar into this. Sprinkle the yeast on the liquid and then leave for a fortnight. Transfer this to your pressure vessel and simply forget about it. If you want to bottle this beer, put a tablespoon of sugar in the bottle, fill with beer and seal. This gives you a really heady drink.

How to pour a beer

You might think this bit silly, but with all the filtered beers around, the trick of pouring from a bottle seems to have been lost. You need a glass big enough to hold the entire contents of the bottle. Slowly present the bottle to the tilted glass and pour slowly. It is important not to let the beer slip back into the bottle because this will agitate the sediment. Pour the whole drink out in one smooth action and leave the last, sediment-rich drop of liquid at the bottom of the bottle.

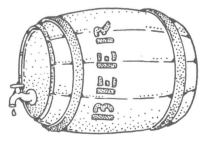

Index

Mayonnaise, 66
Crab Risotto, 72
Cranachan, 161
Cranberry Jelly, 219
Cream of Brussels Sprout Soup, 7
Crusted Salmon in Dill Sauce with Jersey Royals, 93

Dandelion and Nettle Soup, 52
Dandelion Tea, 81
Danish Apple Cake, 196
Dauphinoise Potatoes, 15
December, 224-41
    Menu, 225
Devilled Oysters, 6
Double Gloucester Cheese and Red Onion Tart, 156
Dover Sole with Samphire Tempura, 85
Dried Apricot Jam, 44
Dried-fruit Compote with Brandy, 42
Duck Breasts with Orange and Ginger Sauce, 32

Easy Christmas Cake, 220
Elderberry Cordial, 185
Elderflower Champagne No. 1, 100
Elderflower Champagne No. 2, 101
Elderflower Jelly, 79

Farmhouse Fruit Cake, 43
February, 24-45
    Menu, 25
Fish
    Baked Cod Fillet with Chard, 14
    Baked Mackerel with Apple Stuffing, 54
    Crusted Salmon in Dill Sauce with Jersey Royals, 93
    Dover Sole with Samphire Tempura, 85
    Fish Fritto Misto, 104
    Grilled Sardines with Tomato Sauce, 59
    Lemon Sole Nutty Rolls, 37
    Mackerel Fillets in Oatmeal, 193
    Quick Salmon Pasta with Baby Leaves, 76
    Salmon and Asparagus Parcel, 114
    Salmon Parcels with Sorrel Sauce, 48
    Sea Bass with a Rocket and Butter Sauce, 56
    Sea Bass with Fresh Pesto Sauce, 74
    Sea Trout Pâté with Melba Toast, 109
    Smoked Haddock Kedgeree with Runner Beans, 90
    Smoked Mackeral Pâté, 30
    Smoked Salmon Roulade, 124

Spicy Battered Hake with Parsnip Fries, 27
Three Fish Pie, 177
Winter Fish Pie, 235
Fruit, growing, 262-5
    Apples, 262-3
    Apricots, 263
    Blackberries, 265
    Blackcurrants, 264
    Melons, 264
    Pears, 262-3
    Raspberries, 265
    Strawberries, 265

Ginger, Pear and Walnut Muffins with Ginger Cream, 198
Gooseberry Jam, 141
Greek-style Salad, 130
Green Tomato Chutney, 158
Grilled Sardines with Tomato Sauce, 59

Herb and Courgette Focaccia, 115
Herbs, growing, 257-61
Honey Cake, 78
Honey-glazed Pork Tenderloin, 105

Jam and Jelly
    Blackcurrant Jam, 165
    Bramley Jam, 201
    Cherry Jam, 120
    Cranberry Jelly, 219
    Dried Apricot Jam, 44
    Elderflower Jelly, 79
    Gooseberry Jam, 141
    Pear and Apple Jam, 19
    Plum Jam, 183
    Quince Jam, 223
    Redcurrant Jelly, 184
    Rhubarb Jam, 63
    Rosemary and Mint Jelly, 80
    Strawberry and Apple Jelly, 143
    Strawberry Jam, 98
    Summer Fruit Jam, 140
January, 1-23
    Menu, 1
July, 122-43
    Menu, 123
June, 102-21
    Menu, 103